QUESTS

EDL
GO
BOOK **6**

EDL Go Series Book 6

EDITOR
Elizabeth Zayatz

COMPREHENSION QUESTIONS BY
F. X. Duffy, Jr.

DESIGNER
Mary Dee English

ILLUSTRATORS
John A. McKinzie
Scott Nelson

ART DIRECTOR
Ronald J. Wickham

ISBN 1-55855-666-4

00 99

CONTENTS

MOVIE PALACES

by Arthur Myers

When audiences stepped into the fantastic early movie theaters, they entered a world of pure escape.

"In Xanadu did Kubla Khan a stately pleasure dome decree..."

So opens Samuel Taylor Coleridge's poem, "Kubla Khan." But Kubla Khan should have been living in America during the early twentieth century. Then he would have seen some really fabulous temples of pleasure. He would have experienced architectural achievements that soared beyond anything in historical memory, structures of such brilliance as to be poems in asphalt, miracles on Main Street. At least, a lot of people thought so in those days. We're talking about the movie palaces of the 1920s—as movie theaters were called back then.

1

The Twenties were a time of opposites, historians point out. There were great differences among people in regard to wealth and poverty. The stock market crash of the Thirties was just around the corner, and it would be a great equalizer. But in the Twenties, there were still very, very rich people, and they didn't hide their wealth. The masses of the poor read about the life of the rich with a confusing mixture of envy and wonder—a combination of feelings that added up to longing. "Oh, to live like that, even for a couple of hours," was the secret cry of the common folk.

An answer to this aching need for a more pleasurable life was bursting across the country. At the movies, even the poorest could lose themselves for a time in a dream of wealth, friendship, love, anger, glory—whatever was being shown on the silver screen that day.

In the early 1900s, most picture shows had projected simple "flickers." By the Twenties, the producers, directors, writers, and actors who made movies were taking their work quite seriously as Art. It was up to the people who showed them, the exhibitors, to provide the proper atmosphere for these glorious entertainments. The public certainly was ready. And so, the movie palace was born!

There was a social as well as an entertainment reason for erecting these rather ridiculous structures. One of the leading theater decorators of the day, Harold Rambusch, expressed this theory for the movie palace well when he said:

"In our big modern movie palaces are collections of the most beautiful rugs and furniture that money can produce. No kings or emperors have wandered through more splendid surroundings. In a sense, these theaters are social safety outlets because in the movie palace, the public can enjoy the luxuries usually reserved for only the rich."

Rambusch was called in when Samuel L. Rothafel—one of the most successful showmen of the time—decided to erect a theater. Rothafel's nickname was Roxy, and that was what he called his theater. He told his architect and his decorator that this new theater must look like a palace. It must, at all costs, be a far cry from Roxy's first theater of only 16 years before. This early theater was the back room of a bar in Forest City, Pennsylvania. It was equipped with folding chairs, borrowed from a local funeral home, that were ever in danger of being snatched back in the event of the burial of a popular body.

Built in 1927, the new Roxy Theater had 6,214 seats, which made it the largest movie palace in the world. In fact, it was large enough to shelter the entire population of a small city, visiting firemen included. Its orchestra pit could hold 110 musicians. And there was still room in that monstrously huge pit for three organs. The screen rose and fell on automatic hoists, four times a day, with tidal regularity.

Movies were only part of the entertainment at the theater palace. There was also the stage show, led by the high-kicking Roxyettes, nimble and graceful female dancers. When they were not dancing on the stage, they might be found winding through the audience bearing candles and dressed in white robes. These parades in holy costumes were a favorite part of Easter and Christmas shows. No wonder the Roxy was called "The Cathedral of the Motion Picture."

The audience entered the main hall through a vast area ringed by marble columns, over the largest carpet in the world. It took a regiment of porters working daily to keep the gum off it.

One of the great sights of New York—or at least of Fiftieth Street—was the changing of the ushers. They were carefully selected for manly bearing, sincerity in their performance of duty, and freedom from pimples. Their drill master was a former military officer. At the changing of the ushers ceremony, they would demonstrate difficult drills for those members of the audience who were arriving or leaving.

When Rothafel—the Kubla Khan of Fiftieth Street—gave his marching orders to Rambusch, his decorator, he stated: "I see my theater like the inside of a great bronze bowl: everything in colors of old gold—warm, very rich, marvelous, fabulous!"

And so was born the style that came to be known as Roxy Renaissance. It was copied by theater builders all over the United States. But another style of architecture was also built on Main Street sites. It was called the atmospheric style, and its leading architect was a man named John Eberson.

Born in Austria, Eberson loved the world of make-believe. His movie-theater structures were pure escape. The scenes were a marvel of decorating: ceilings that showed skies forever blue and walls with vines forever green. Eberson himself described some of his achievements as follows:

"...a glorious festival under a moonlight sky...an Italian garden, a Persian court, a Spanish patio, a mysterious Egyptian temple yard...where friendly stars twinkle and white clouds drift."

The effect of these scenes on crowds soaked in rain

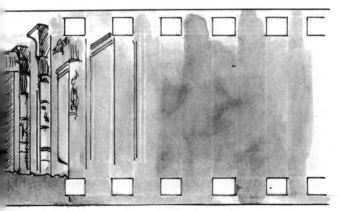

and problems of the real world was startling—and made for wonderful attendance and long lines at the box office.

These fantastic piles of architecture were by no means limited to the nation's huge centers of population. Small cities as well could boast of their entertainment palaces, and they certainly did. An example is the Assyrian-type Missouri Theater, in St. Joseph, Missouri. The Missouri had a ceiling painted to give the effect of a sky showing behind the corners of a great desert tent. Loew's State in Syracuse, New York, introduced India, with elephants plodding and slave girls squirming around its immense walls.

Some theaters were decorated in a local style. The Kimo Theater in Albuquerque, New Mexico, for example, had Navajo blankets hung along the walls. A further nice touch was provided by cattle skulls arranged over the stage. Some architects and decorators went in more for the foreign effect, an example being the Chinese fire-breathing dragon that livened the curtain of a theater in Plainfield, New Jersey.

But all things must end. When the great market crash struck in 1929, the fate of the big theaters was sealed. Mass taste changed—slightly for the better, some observers say. People wanted simpler styles: blue mirrors, frosted glass, and shiny metal stair rails.

At the same time, talking pictures came in, and blew the musicians out of their pits and the organists out of their lofts. Live talent disappeared from the stages, and popcorn became much more important to the entertainment business than painted ceilings, banjos, choruses, and high kickers.

Few movie houses were built in the Thirties and Forties, and in the Fifties the death blow struck—television. Today most people see a movie—when they do—in a small, snug, new auditorium. Or if it is one left over from the old days, it's usually a dreary place haunted by the ghosts of wandering ushers with bewildered theater owners counting the sketchy attendance.

The ghosts of the old movie palaces themselves haunt the more run-down sections of towns all over the country. A paint store here, a second-hand furniture establishment there, and many, many a parking lot stand on the sites once graced by movie palaces.

The splendid, short life of the movie palace can be tied up in the experience of one person, the movie star Gloria Swanson. She figured in the birth and death of the Roxy. The opening show at the new theater was to be one of her movies, and Roxy himself was showing her around the new place. At one point she suddenly danced through the workmen's litter, took a stick, and carved in some wet plaster the words: DEAR ROXY - I LOVE YOU - GLORIA.

Roxy was so touched that he gave orders that the words should be left there forever. But forever is a long time. Thirty-three years was more like it. In 1960, the famous Roxy was being torn down to make room for an office building, and the unfeeling wrecking crew smashed the gold-leafed autograph to dusty bits. Nothing lasts forever.

The Meteor

Part 1
by Kay Jordan

For years, Henry Weatherbee had lived for the day he could get even with Franklin "Moose" Allen and the rest of the boys in his neighborhood. Actually, the boys liked Henry. The problem was Henry's brains. He was smarter than all of them put together, and they knew it. So, long ago, they had decided that Henry was weird. Still, Henry had his uses.

When they were in grade school, the boys made Henry read every note Mr. Bradley, the school principal, sent home to their parents. If Henry said the note meant trouble, the note never got home. Then they decided that Henry shouldn't enter any of their playground contests since he couldn't do anything but be smart. Instead, they forced Henry to be judge. Now if those tasks gave Henry a sense of achievement, the results of his work were not always pleasant. He would have gladly traded being brilliant for a little peace.

8

After years of having jokes played on him, Henry sees his chance to get even with Moose and the gang.

9

But peace was impossible for Henry because he lived next door to Moose and across the street from Peter "Stringbean" Crawford. Whenever Moose would get a note to take home from the principal, and that was often, he would get mad at Henry for the bad news. Moose's way of dealing with anger was to throw Henry in the local gooseberry bushes, then tear up the note.

Stringbean posed a different problem. He was always thinking up contests that often got the gang in trouble. Also, Stringbean didn't like to lose. His contest to see who could spit the farthest was a typical example.

As judge, Henry decided Stringbean was the poorest spitter in the gang. Stringbean got mad and spit on Henry—but not before he had spit on Mr. Bradley's shoes, much to Stringbean's and the principal's amazement. As the boys were leaving the principal's office, Mr. Bradley asked Henry why he let the others get in trouble.

Henry pondered the question. Would Mr. Bradley understand how it felt to be hoisted up the flagpole and threatened with having to kiss Daisy Brown if you dared come down too soon? Henry doubted it. Besides, if he told on the boys, they wouldn't play with him. That would leave him only the girls as friends. Henry didn't like feeling alien, and he didn't like playing with the girls, especially Daisy Brown. So Henry only shrugged his shoulders in answer to the principal's question.

While elementary school was bad for Henry, junior high was somewhat better. The gang discovered girls while Henry discovered science. He spent hours trying to decide which frontier of exploration he wished to conquer. He gave considerable thought to whether his picture would get on the cover of *Time* faster if he cured the common cold or discovered another planet in the solar system.

Finally Henry decided to become the world's greatest astronomer. Soon he had a new telescope, and he invited Moose and Stringbean over to inspect it. They thought it was so terrific that Henry couldn't get near his instrument for two weeks. Moose and Stringbean were always coming over to use it. They were trying to peer past sheer curtains into "Looney" Hazel's bedroom window.

Henry decided to get around this problem by taking the telescope to school, only to have Moose steal it from him. Moose tried to sight it on the girls' gym, but got caught. That, of course, made Moose angry and he blamed Henry. Next gym class, Moose pulled off Henry's shirt and pants and threw him out into the hall wearing only his underwear.

After the boys entered high school, Henry thought it would be safe to pursue his career as a scholar. Stringbean and the other gearheads disappeared into the shop classes, leaving Henry to select friends from students he met in various laboratories. But Henry still had two problems, and the first was still Moose.

Moose's main interest was to make the all-city football team. Unfortunately, somewhere Moose got the idea of going to college, and decided to follow his original plan for getting through school: copying Henry's homework and test answers.

Henry's second problem was girls. Henry tried to oppose the gang's idea that he had to take out every stray girl who was a friend of the gang's steadies. When Henry tried to discuss his objections, the boys threatened to smash his test tubes. Henry gave in and entertained the girls, but the dates were never successful.

One of Henry's dates was so big that he almost had to crowbar her into his tiny car. Another spent the evening trying to sign him up for her favorite singer's fan club. A third ate the meal he bought her, then went off on the back of a motorcycle with a total stranger—much to Henry's relief. After several other similar dates, Henry decided that all his dates had one thing in common: the space between their ears was filled with asphalt.

One awful evening at the local drive-in was spent with Moose's cousin, who filed her nails throughout the whole movie. Henry later complained to Moose.

"Well, what do you want?" Moose asked.

"A brain, Moose. A girl with a brain," Henry answered.

"A brain? What can you do with a brain, Henry?"

Henry considered the source and didn't answer.

Then Henry's long-awaited chance to get even with Moose came from an unexpected source—chemistry class. He had managed to get Moose through biology, but chemistry was a different story. During their first test, Henry worked the problems wrong as Moose copied the answers from him. Then Henry went back and changed the answers.

In their first laboratory class, Henry quickly noticed that Moose had no idea what to do. So

Henry decided to help his friend. He told Moose that since oxygen plus hydrogen make water, Moose would be able to make a water bomb by holding a hydrogen-filled balloon over a burner. Moose's singed eyebrows were the hit of the period. Henry enjoyed the sight so much that he didn't even mind spending fifteen minutes after school in one of Moose's hammerlocks.

In the next lab class, Moose happened to ask Henry why there was a chain hanging from the ceiling. Henry told him that one pull would let out laughing gas, which would put an end to the lab. Never one to pass up a joke, Moose pulled the chain and got soaking wet from the emergency shower. Henry was still laughing when Moose threw him into the girls' gym to show his extreme displeasure.

Even with Henry's help—or maybe because of it—Moose was failing chemistry. That meant he would get benched in football. Desperate for a miracle, Moose decided to enter the science fair. His main problem was that he had no ideas for a science project. The chemistry teacher suggested a carbon experiment, but then refused to accept a scrapbook of football plays traced on carbon paper. She said that was not what she meant by carbon experiment.

Moose frantically turned to Henry for help. Henry might have helped if only Moose hadn't played one last trick. In the library, he stuck a sign on Henry's back that said, "Kiss me, Daisy." Everyone laughed when Henry walked up to the counter to check out his books.

Henry decided to get even once and for all. His first thought was to send Moose to a radiation dump, telling him to steal a lead box for his science project. Henry laughed at the vision of a hairless tackle, but he decided that idea would send him to jail.

Henry decided to work on a plan that would injure Moose without killing him. He pondered selling Moose on the idea of a solar project by instructing him to observe the sun at high noon for an hour each day. Henry liked to think of Moose going through life with a seeing-eye dog until he felt sorry for the dog.

Finally, Henry had the perfect idea! Moose wanted something simple and digging up a meteor was simple. Of course, Henry knew of no meteor, but he did know of an old sewer block, buried out by the rock quarry. Moose would never know the difference. After a hard rain, the sewage would back up behind the block, and Henry would have his revenge. Since Moose would need help to loosen the block, Stringbean and the others would have to come along—which was all the better to Henry's way of thinking.

Henry worked on the plan until it was perfect. Then he sat back and waited. Within a couple of days, Moose was again begging him for help. Henry smiled.

"Boy, do I have a great idea for you, Moose! I know of this meteor..."

End of Part 1

The Meteor

Part 2
by Kay Jordan

Henry's evening begins with a practical joke and ends at the police station.

"Henry, are you sure there's a genuine meteor buried out near the old rock-quarry site?" Moose asked for the hundredth time.

"I'm positive," Henry answered. "Whenever a meteor lands, everyone fights over who owns it. Usually the courts get involved. So, when this meteor landed, the city leaders decided to keep its arrival quiet."

"But why bury it?"

"Protection, Moose, protection," Henry answered. "Meteors are valuable. Everyone who knew about the meteor swore to keep quiet. I'm breaking a supreme trust by telling you. But you're my friend and you need a science project. Besides, we'll only borrow the meteor until after the science fair."

"But why can't I just dig up any old rock and say it's a meteor?" Moose asked. "Remember the time we found a bird's skull and said it was prehistoric? We almost got away with it too."

"Almost doesn't count, Moose," Henry reminded the football player. "Just get Stringbean and his pick-up truck, three or four of the gang, shovels, and a towing chain. I'll bring the flashlight."

"Tonight?"

"No, it's supposed to rain hard tonight. We'll do it tomorrow," Henry said.

"Won't the rain make it a muddy mess out there?" Moose asked.

"Moose, trust me," Henry said. "Yes, it will be muddy, but we have no choice. Just pick me up tomorrow night at 9:30 P.M."

"OK, Henry, and thanks."

The next night, Stringbean headed the pick-up out to the city property near the quarry. Moose and Henry sat in the front with Stringbean, and three other gang members sat in the back.

"When we get there, you'll have to dig until you hit metal," Henry told them. "Then I'll identify the top of the dome."

"Why aren't you digging, Henry?" Stringbean asked.

"I thought up the project," Henry reminded him. "Besides, I'll do better to drive the truck, since your strength is superior to mine."

"Henry, will we be guilty of doing something criminal?" Stringbean asked.

"Well, you could say we're trespassing and stealing government property," Henry answered. "Use your own judgment. Is it any worse than the time you guys made off with the tombstone from the cemetery and planted it in the principal's yard?"

"Man, that was cool. We're OK," Stringbean decided.

"Yeah," Moose and the others agreed.

Henry directed Stringbean to the spot. Then Henry passed out shovels and the gang began to dig. He held the flashlight close enough for them to see where they were digging, but not close enough for them to be able to see the sewer block's lid. When they called for more light, Henry told them, "I don't want to take a chance of this light reacting with the meteor's nitrogen."

Finally, after an hour of digging, Moose hit metal. Stringbean looked at Henry and warned, "We'd better get something out of all this."

"You will, Stringbean. Believe me, you will," Henry assured him.

The boys cleaned off the block's top, then got out of the ditch so Henry could inspect it. Then they connected the towing chain to the handle on top of the block. The meteor, according to Henry, was inside the block.

"Now remember, guys," Henry said as he headed for the truck. "As soon as the lid comes off, all of you reach over and grab it. We don't want the lid swinging wildly. Then toss it aside and grab the meteor."

As he walked to the truck, Henry wondered if the past day's heavy rains had brought the city's system to overflowing. He climbed into the pick-up, took one last look at the boys, and smiled. Then he turned the starter key and drove the truck forward.

The sound of the breaking sewer block was music to Henry's ears, as were the screams and yells from the gang. They danced around trying to miss the sewage bursting out of the broken block. The smell almost made Henry sick. The others swore so loudly that Henry knew it was against his better judgment to stay, but he was laughing too hard to drive off. Henry locked the doors, lay back, and howled as the soaked boys banged on the windows, first pleading and then threatening him. Every slam of the fist only served to remind Henry of the times he had banged on the gym's locker-room door in his birthday suit.

Henry's fun was interrupted by the flashing lights of three vehicles: two police cars and a city inspection truck. Several police officers lined up the gang against the truck. Despite the rest of the gang's threats to kill him the moment the police left, Henry still couldn't stop laughing. The expression on the boys' faces was worth risking death or the gooseberry bushes.

The rest of the night wasn't such fun. Henry alone had the honor of riding to the station with the police. The other boys smelled so bad that they were made to travel in Stringbean's pick-up, which was sandwiched between the two police cars. When they arrived at the station, the police officers made them yell their names from the truck because they smelled too awful to take into the station. Henry had to call their parents and ask them to bring clean clothes to the station.

Before the night was over, the authorities had filed criminal trespass charges against Henry and the other boys. No one could give them an argument, since the police wouldn't get close enough to the boys to hear their side of the story. The police let the parents hose off their sons in the station yard, and then sent them home. The boys and their parents were to meet at Henry's house for a neighborhood meeting.

Henry knew the boys were angry, but he hadn't realized how mad the parents would be when they found out what had happened. Everyone was concerned about Moose's future. He was the high school football hero, and no one wanted to see criminal charges pressed against him. Then all the adults worried about legal fees. Henry decided that having everyone yell at him was the worst punishment he'd ever faced. He took it bravely until his own father started in on him.

"Henry, I thought you were above this sort of thing," his father said. "I condemn the whole idea. I don't understand how you could do such an awful thing to your friends."

The sight of his own father turning against him made Henry furious. Henry yelled back for the first time in his life.

"You're my father," Henry said, "but all you care about is Moose and the others. No one ever cared what happened to me. What about all the awful things they did to me? I'm supposed to sit back and take it 'cause I'm just 'poor Henry'? Well, I took it for years and tonight I got back. It was nothing more than they deserved."

"Henry, what are you talking about?" Moose's mother asked. "I always thought you boys were friends."

"What kind of friends throw you into the gooseberry bushes and hoist you up a flagpole?" Henry went on to list almost every prank the boys had pulled on him over the years.

"Are those things all true?" Moose's mother asked the gang in amazement.

"Naw," Moose said and the others shook their heads. But Stringbean, always looking for an argument, spoke up, "Henry, why didn't you deck us or tell us off? We picked on you only because we knew we could."

"And that made it all right?" Henry shot back.

"For me it did," Stringbean said. "Pick or get picked on. You're as big as any of us. You don't have to be a wimp."

"Well, tonight the wimp got you back. That's the way I fight."

"Well, it's a sneaky, stinking, rotten way to fight!" Stringbean said.

"Stinking isn't the word," Moose added, and everyone laughed.

Moose's mother stood up and said, "It's late. Tomorrow we can see if the boys can clean up the mess they made and somehow pay for any damage. If they do, maybe the city will drop the charges against the boys."

As the parents said good-night, the gang punched Henry lightly and smiled at him. Henry realized that they liked him better now that they realized he wasn't such a wimp after all.

As Moose was leaving, he put his arm around Henry's shoulders and said, "Henry, if I get benched, I'm going to smash your face."

"You do, Moose," Henry answered, "and you'll flunk chemistry whether we get out of this or not. Then you still won't get to play football."

"Deal, Henry?" Moose asked hopefully. "If I lay off on the jokes, and get the others to lay off, will you really help me?"

"Add no dates to that and you've got a deal," Henry answered.

"Not even if I find a brain for you?"

"No dates, Moose."

"It's a deal. No jokes and no dates," Moose agreed sadly and the two shook hands. Suddenly Moose had an idea. "Hey, Henry, that's it, a brain."

"What are you talking about, Moose?"

"I'll stick a brain in a bottle and enter it in the science fair!" Moose said excitedly.

"Whose brain?" Henry asked suspiciously.

"Doesn't matter. One probably looks like any other. I'll buy a calf's brain at the grocery store and say it's human."

Henry shook his head. "It'll never work, Moose." After a moment's thought he added, "But it's worth a try."

Working mothers have to balance their job responsibilities with their family lives.

HIGH-PROFILE WORKING MOTHERS

Many working mothers rely on day-care centers for the care of their young children during working hours. Others hire private babysitters or rely on childcare help from family members, like husbands, aunts, and grandparents. There are some women in the workforce who balance successful careers in the spotlight with family and motherhood. Many of these "high-profile" mothers have the benefit of housekeepers, helpful mates, and other supports. Still, because of their harried schedules, they often go to great lengths to keep their home and work lives in balance. But because of the many rewards, they say they wouldn't have it any other way.

As Chicago TV reporter Dorothy Tucker accepted a community service award at a South Side church, a joyful shriek broke through the sound of the clapping. "Mama!" a proud voice cried out.

"It was a great moment," the WBBM-TV reporter says of the joyful noise made by her son, Trevor, who was nearly 2 years old at the time.

Tucker's triumph was one of those precious

moments when a high-profile career pleasantly happens at the same time as motherhood. It also was the kind of moment, career women in the spotlight say, that helps them realize what's really important—family.

The most common thought regarding high-powered mothers is that their enjoyment of life in the fast lane is overshadowed by the things that go wanting in their personal lives. But that's rarely the case for caring women with demanding careers and families, too. For one thing, their jobs afford them benefits and opportunities they otherwise would not have. "One of the best things about this job is that when my kids come to see mom at the office, they are wandering around the White House," says Anna Perez, press secretary to the first lady.

Because she has a job in the spotlight, Perez says, "My family sort of followed my career around the world on CNN." What also comforted her was that her husband, Ted Sims, head of Howard University's film screening room, and her sister-in-law, Mattie Sims, were at home to pinch-hit for her.

Doing what they have to do means, in some cases, that high-profile moms cart their children with them to business meetings. The son of state Rep. Sundra Escott-Russell, 37, D-Birmingham, is well known around the Alabama State Capitol. One-year-old David Aaron Russell, Jr., accompanies his mother to committee meetings and is sometimes seen peeking around the Capitol pillars. "He's good about sitting in meetings," she says. "If he gets upset, I'll just give him a bottle. When I take a couple of minutes out to hug him and hold him, he's satisfied."

Other mothers with important career responsibilities tell almost the same stories. Vanessa Bell Calloway, who acted in the hit film, *Coming to America*, took her week-and-a-half-old daughter, Ashley, with her to try out for a part in *Boyz N the Hood*. "I was nursing and couldn't be away from Ashley that long," she says. "So I packed her and the housekeeper up and we all went to the try-outs together....I'm not leaving my baby and I'm not giving up my career."

This double responsibility of career and family leads to some harried moments, but putting things into their order of importance helps mothers smooth out the rough edges of their lives.

"The first rule for me is my children come first. This helps me make decisions very clearly and without any sense of guilt," says Dr. Mary Schmidt Campbell, cultural chief of New York City. The woman who oversees the world's largest and most famous arts community gives equal weight to lunch dates with her son, Sekou, 15, and husband, Dr. George Campbell, 45, who heads the New York-based National Action Council for Minorities in Engineering, Inc., and to work-related responsibilities.

"I usually mark their dates into my calendar," Dr. Campbell says of family lunch dates. "I can't afford to leave things to chance." She even sometimes rides the subway to the day-care center during lunch to check up on 1-year-old Britt.

Taking a different approach is Shirley Tyus, 41, one of four black female pilots at United Airlines. The second officer, who flies Boeing 727 jets, is out of town an average of 15 days a month. But when she is home in Washington, D.C., with her husband, Kofi, an artist with a greeting card business, and daughters, Ofosuwa, 4, and Akosua, 8, she makes dinner for her ravenous family, using her daughters as kitchen helpers.

"I have to let them be a part of day-to-day duties when time is tight," says Tyus, who is studying to be a first officer. "I try not to shortchange my children because of my dreams and career goals. I'll take the 8-year-old aside and say, 'This is your day.' And sometimes, my husband and I will just snatch moments and go bike riding."

In dividing time between career and family, mothers have learned to be good planners. Dr. Campbell avoids wasting time in endless searches for any needed items by insisting on neatness at home and having everything in its place. TV reporter Tucker prepares meals and freezes them for reheating later.

"This way, I can fix it, eat it, and we're done eating in 15 minutes," she says. "Then I have more time to spend with my son, reading or watching a Sesame Street video together, or playing and singing songs." She and her husband, Tony Wilkins, who directs new business marketing for a Chicago firm, bought a dishwasher so they would not waste precious time standing over a sink while Trevor cried for attention.

Tucker and other mothers in the spotlight make more family time by attending fewer parties, weekend speaking dates, and other events that keep them from their families. Putting family first also means less time for friends and entertainment.

"I tell my girlfriends I can meet them for brunch, lunch, or munch, but come 4 o'clock, I have to be home," says Vanessa Bell Calloway. "That's when my husband gets home and the three of us spend time together."

Even after trimming the fat from their schedules, these busy women say that their lives would be a nightmare without a support team.

It's Tucker's husband who must get up and help when she gets a 6 A.M. call to go to the scene of a fire. "Sometimes I think he takes a little joy in having to wake me up and say, "Honey, there's a fire,' because he's usually the first one out of the house," says the TV reporter. Her husband must on occasion reschedule early morning meetings. His tennis dates and evening plans are sometimes changed if Tucker must work late to do a story on a fire, a menacing tornado, or other late-breaking news.

With Dr. Campbell, on the other hand, the entire family pitches in. She missed one important meeting of her committee to give birth to Britt. But for the next meeting, six weeks after Britt's birth, her oldest son, Garikai, 21, traveled with her to Washington, D.C., to stay with his young brother while Dr. Campbell ran the meeting.

Campbell also sings the praises of her husband, who takes the children mountain climbing and picks Britt up from the day-care center when she has important work to do. "There is no way I could have a high-profile position if my husband did not share in the role of parenting," Campbell says, echoing the feelings of others in her position.

White House press secretary Anna Perez says her husband is also a bedrock of support. While she admits the demands of her job "sometimes can get old" for him, she knows she can always count on his backing and strength. "Ted is the perfect blend of old-fashioned and modern," she explains. "He's old-fashioned in the sense that the kids really do see him as the head of the house and modern in the sense that we know it's a partnership."

The challenges are gigantic. But when high-profile mothers finally get a moment to reflect on their experiences, they say they would change little. High-powered women are recharged by their work, enjoy motherhood, and say their careers make them better at parenting.

"Because of those years at the Studio Museum in Harlem, both of my older sons have a great understanding of the history and richness of their culture," says Dr. Campbell, who directed the Studio Museum for 10 years before becoming the Big Apple's cultural boss. "From the viewpoint of the Department of Cultural Arts, my sons have had a vivid view of the city's cultural life."

What's also rewarding are moments like the one pilot Tyus had when her son Andre, 22, handed her a touching letter. "Your achievements have provided me with the perfect role model in everything I am trying to achieve in my own life," he wrote.

Reprinted by permission of EBONY Magazine, © 1991 by Johnson Publishing Company, Inc.

A terrifying nightmare comes true for the crew of...

The Phantom

by Sarah Lang

Anyone who did submarine duty during World War II has a story to tell. My tale, though, is weird, even when compared to the strangest of battle accounts. Time and again, I have pondered my experience for long hours. Now I have decided to set it down for others to read and judge.

I served my country as a naval captain. Toward the end of the war, I was given command of a new submarine. It was capable of diving deeper than any other submarine and carried a new type of torpedo. My responsibility was to sink as many enemy ships as possible. My crew and I succeeded beyond anyone's expectations.

The submarine was able to cruise at a depth so

29

great that the enemy usually didn't pick us up on their radar equipment. At the right moment, we'd rise to the proper firing level and fire the torpedoes. Because the torpedoes seemed to come from nowhere, our submarine became known among the enemy as *The Phantom.*

When the vibrations from the last torpedo hitting its target would die down, I'd give the order to ascend. *The Phantom* would break through the water. We'd rush onto the drenched deck and see several ships burning on the ocean surface. Other ships would be fleeing the scene, their officers never able to catch a glimpse of us through the smoke and fire.

My crew and I felt great amazement at our good luck in those first months. Oh, the crew was excellent—the men really knew their jobs. They were experts at using navigation instruments and they were accurate in hitting the targets. However, a submarine doesn't usually go as long as we did without being spotted and attacked. In the calm between raids, we always wondered when our luck would run out.

If any of those other submarine stories you've read tell you that war is all excitement and glory, don't believe them. Sure, we felt great when we pulled into port after a successful run. All the big shots would come and pat us on the back. Our friends would take us out for celebrations. In no time, though, we would again be confined within the tiny space of the submarine, twitching with nervousness as we watched enemy ships on the radar screen. We found it very hard to sleep or relax.

Under the strain, we began to get on each other's nerves.

This may seem odd, but the longer *The Phantom*'s good fortune continued, the worse life on the submarine became for us. We knew the odds. Our luck would have to run out soon. Would we be blasted in this mission? If not, surely we would be bombed in the next.

We began having nightmares. Even though we knew we were fighting for a good cause, the thought of all the people we'd killed was hard for us to accept. None of us wanted to be in a war, and we certainly didn't want to kill anyone. Yet that was our job during the war. Imagine doing daily the one thing that is the most forbidden, and you can understand why we were having nightmares. In these dreams, *The Phantom* was bombed or we received other horrible punishments. The worst nightmares were those in which we were trapped at the bottom of the sea forever.

The turning point in our luck came one day while the submarine was in port for minor repairs. I was called to a top-secret meeting by my commander. He began by congratulating me on my great success. Then he informed me that *The Phantom* had been chosen for a special mission. I was to pilot the submarine into the most dangerous of enemy waters and wipe out a whole fleet of battleships. With the enemy's fleet destroyed, our side would almost certainly win the war at sea.

I agreed to the plan. Anything that brought us closer to victory—closer to the end of war—seemed like a good idea to me. As *The Phantom* left port, I shared the news of the special mission with the crew. The men were glad for the chance to be heroes—even if they never saw shore again. But as we approached enemy territory, the nightmares began to haunt us again.

As soon as we actually entered dangerous waters, I gave the order to submerge. We were to sit near the ocean bottom until all the enemy battleships were in sight. Then we were to rise to the correct depth and fire.

Down, down, down we went, into the dark and mysterious depths of the sea. The lower we sank, the more gloomy the crew's mood became. As many times as we'd done this before, the men were jumpy. We all wished that we could just go into battle and be done with it. My lieutenant, Sam, usually a practical, clear-minded fellow, said the ocean floor was calling us to our doom.

I ignored the crew's bad nerves. I told everyone, except the few men needed to stand watch, to take a rest. You could have hard a pin drop in the submarine that night, although I think most of the men just pretended to sleep. They were all thinking about what the next day would bring.

I was just dozing off when my lieutenant came to tell me that the enemy battleships were showing on the radar screen. I wanted to be positive before waking the men, so I checked the screen myself. There they were, sitting like ducks. I dared not sound the battle alarm. The men were awakened one by one. When they were at their posts, I gave the order to ascend.

To my horror, nothing happened. *The Phantom*

didn't move. What was going on? I knew the submarine's power supply was still good, because we had lights. But we couldn't seem to go anywhere. I took a few crew members and we went over every part of the submarine. We couldn't find a thing wrong. Then my lieutenant remembered the porthole. The older submarines didn't have a porthole, so you could never see what was around you in the ocean, but this new submarine did. I ordered *The Phantom*'s outside lights to be turned on and rushed to that porthole.

Through that little pane of glass opening on to the ocean floor, I saw the strangest scene of my life. Look at your hand. Now, imagine that your palm and your fingers have turned into flowers, the most brightly colored flowers you've ever seen—yellow, red, purple, and green. That, reader, is what I saw through the porthole. I stood back and let the others have a look. We all came to the same conclusion— those flowery hands were holding the submarine at the bottom of the sea.

That's not hard to say now. At the time, though, the idea that we were stuck in a bed of half-human hands of flowers was impossible to admit. I'm afraid I was a bit rough when I told Sam to prepare himself for a swim to get a closer look at those flowers.

Sam quickly dressed in his wet suit and aqualung. His face above that black suit was white as chalk, and no wonder. If we were right and those flowers were gripping the submarine like hands, what might they do to Sam?

We let Sam into the submarine's special outside chamber. It slowly filled with water, allowing Sam to adjust to the water pressure of the ocean depths. Then he entered the sea. The minutes ticked by slowly in the submarine while we waited for Sam to come back—if he was going to.

Sam returned safely, and I can only tell you what he told us. You may choose to believe it or not. He said that *The Phantom* was resting on the huge bed of weird flowers we'd seen through the porthole. They were indeed shaped like hands, some more gigantic than a tall person. The enormous fingers of each flower-hand were clutching the submarine to keep it from floating away. The fingers of some of the hands had parted from the submarine to let Sam in and out. They didn't menace Sam, but he was badly shaken by the alien sight.

The Phantom lay in the spot for seventy-two hours, unable to move. All of us thought that our terrible nightmare of being trapped forever at the bottom of the sea had come true. Each of us pondered how and why the sea kept us in the grip of this weird garden. Periodically we would try to ascend, but had no luck.

At the end of three days, we tried the engine once again. Shocked and relieved, I felt *The Phantom* move. I glanced out the porthole and had another surprise: no flowers were to be seen. We surfaced and radioed for instructions, only to find that the war was over!

I believe those hands were stopping *The Phantom* from doing any more killing. I have heard of stranger things. To this day, I don't understand where the flowers came from. But then, I don't understand war either.

There were fourteen women in the expedition. Ten went up, but only eight returned from...

THE SUMMIT OF ANNAPURNA

by Arthur Myers

"There were so many avalanches yesterday. It gives you a scary feeling. You hear a roar; you see a cloud of snow, watch it get bigger, and realize with a sickening certainty that it could reach you. You run for shelter. Then you feel the tent shake from the spray and realize you're still alive. Relief."

Those words were spoken by Arlene Blum into a tape recorder on October 8, 1978. She was at an elevation of 18,500 feet (5,639 meters) near the top of the tenth-highest mountain in the world—Annapurna I, in the Himalayan mountains of Nepal.

Arlene was the leader of an expedition of fourteen women. They were determined to be the first women's team to climb one of the world's fourteen 26,504-foot (8,078-meter) mountains.

Most of the team was from the San Francisco Bay area. They had formed a group called American Women's Himalayan Expeditions. Their motto was: "A woman's place is on top." They had raised $80,000 for the expedition with the aid of the National Geographic Society and by selling T-shirts with their motto on the front.

They were educated women, with a variety of accomplishments aside from mountain climbing. They were not all young by any means. Joan Firey, an artist from Seattle, passed her fiftieth birthday on Annapurna. Arlene Blum, 31, was a scientist; Irene Miller, 41, was also a scientist, as was Vera Watson, 44. Piro Kramar, 40, was a doctor; Vera Komarkova, 35, was an expert in high-altitude plants; Liz Klobusicky, 33, was a professor from Spokane, Washington.

There were also two motion-picture experts, a young woman whose responsibility was to manage the base camp, and two college students experienced in mountain climbing. An international flavor was provided by Wanda Rutkiewicz, a well-known Polish climber, and Alison Chadwick-Onyszkiewicz, a British artist from Leeds.

In Nepal, the team added Nepalese high-altitude porters, cooks, and helpers of other sorts. They brought and bought six tons of food, fuel, and equipment, and set out for their base camp, 80 miles (129 kilometers) away. They looked like a small army moving along the high plateau—250 Nepalese and 14 Western women with their eyes and thoughts on the summit, 26,504 feet up.

They set up their base camp of red and green tents at 14,200 feet (4,328 meters). The summit of Annapurna loomed 12,300 feet (3,749 meters) above them—nearly two and a half vertical miles (4 kilometers). During the ascent they would set up six other camps at higher and higher elevations.

Near the base camp was a rock memorial bearing the names of seven climbers who had lost their lives trying to conquer the nightmarish avalanches, sheer drops, and jagged peaks of Annapurna I. The women prayed silently that no names from their group would be added to that menacing stone.

They established Camp I on schedule. It was at 16,500 feet (5,029 meters) on the mountain. It was a beginning, and it gave them great satisfaction.

Back and forth they trudged between Camp I and the base camp. They carried anything and everything portable to Camp I, setting up supplies to maintain a base for the attack on the remote reaches above. Then the mountain showed its teeth. Arlene Blum wrote in the *National Geographic* magazine:

"It snowed a lot last night. This morning, Vera, Irene, and I went up to decide on a location for Camp II. We chopped steps in the ice to make the going safer. The glacier rose steeply. We cut over to a rocky place and continued. Above the rock, the route went up ice under 6 inches (15 centimeters) of snow. Carrying a heavy load, Irene broke trail and was weary at 18,500 feet (5,639 meters). Three times I spent half an hour untangling rope."

And the next day she spoke into her tape recorder:

"I started reading *The Thorn Birds* last night. Finished the whole thing—530 pages—about 3:30 A.M. Good escapism to be on the hot Australian plains for a few hours. All night I knocked snow off the tent. Closing my book, I heard a crash. Snow had brought down the mess tent."

Then began the work of carrying supplies to Camp II. The route was even more menacing. In some places they groped along a knife blade of ice no more than 4 inches (10 centimeters) wide with gigantic drops to either side. To lose one's grip would send a climber smashing 100 feet (30 meters) down to an icy tomb.

Now they peered upward to a spot 21,000 feet (6,400 meters) high, where they planned to establish Camp III. To get there, they had to cross a thin rib of ice. They called it Dutch Rib, after a Dutch expedition that had gone that way in 1977. It was steep and dangerous. The narrow rib ran for more than a mile (1.6 kilometers). Avalanches swept across it. To get to Dutch Rib, the climbers had to cross a thousand feet (305 meters) of snow and ice, boosting their bodies and equipment upward at an angle of 50 to 60 degrees. It was a discouraging and perilous stretch of mountain.

Arlene Blum turned to their Nepalese guides. "Well," she asked, "do you think we should try?"

"Yes," their leader replied. "There is no safer way."

But before they could ascend, the avalanches began in earnest. Arlene pulled the advance party back from Camp II to Camp I. It snowed so hard they had to shovel every few minutes to keep the tents from caving in. It was days before they could move. Everybody kept talking about going to K.C.'s Pie Shop in the Nepalese capital city of Kathmandu. Finally the snow stopped, and it was time to mount the attack on Dutch Rib.

Annie Whitehouse, 21, a student at the University of Wyoming, and Arlene carried loads up to Camp

IIIA. They decided to establish this site on Dutch Rib before pushing on another 600 feet (183 meters) to Camp III. They walked across the remains of a gigantic avalanche that had smashed down to the left of the rib. They knew another avalanche could start at any time. As they ascended the rib, Arlene could only think, "If I die, I die."

At times they had to climb 60- or 70-degree slopes of ice. Then the going became easier, and they began to enjoy climbing the challenging face. The view across the peaks and valleys of the Himalayas filled them with an aching wonder.

On September 26, almost a month after their first view of Annapurna from their base camp, Arlene confided to her tape recorder: "It's really getting scary." The vibration of avalanches was now a common experience. One monstrous slide buried an entire store of their equipment.

On October 8, they clawed their way to the site of Camp IV. The altitude was 23,200 feet (7,071 meters), about 3,000 feet (914 meters) below the summit. Arlene recorded:

"We've had a lot of really hard climbing, but it's almost over. A lot of people would have split by now, inventing excuses. We're not being heroes; many of us are afraid. But we're doing it."

Now it was time to select teams for the summit. For the first team, Arlene picked Irene Miller, Vera Komarkova, and Piro Kramar. They and three Nepalese went up to establish Camp V, the highest camp, at 24,200 feet (7,376 meters). The loads were heavy, the air was thin, and the temperature hovered at 20° F below zero (-29° C). At the last moment,

Piro Kramar found a hole in her glove. Her finger was white, frostbitten. Piro was an eye doctor who performed operations, and she decided that she needed her finger more than seeing Annapurna's summit. Piro stayed behind.

As the first team began their climb to the summit, Arlene began to climb down the mountain. She finally saw a black speck above Camp II. It was Christy Tews, the camp manager, waiting for her. When Arlene was 50 feet (15 meters) from Christy, she ran through the snow, yelling, "Did they make it?" Christy nodded. They threw their arms around each other and sobbed. A woman's place *was* on top!

But tears of another kind—tears of sorrow—were on the way. The second summit team of Vera Watson and Alison Chadwick-Onyszkiewicz had set out from Camp V. Their Nepalese guide had gotten altitude sickness and had to come down. The women were reported missing a little while later. With powerful binoculars, the people below searched Annapurna's peak, but there was no sign of the two women. Then two Nepalese guides went up to look for them. They found them dead, their bodies roped together. Apparently, one had slipped just below Camp V. Both fell 1,500 feet (457 meters) down a steep incline of snow and ice.

Their companions carved their names in the rock memorial at the foot of Annapurna. As the women stood before the memorial, their emotions a mixture of triumph and grief, they heard the roar of another avalanche—the sound of Annapurna.

A visit to a farm turns into a nightmare.

The Blue Heron Farm

by Judith P. Gordon and Rosemary P. Ritvo

"Look at that," Steve said suddenly. "A genuine Martian just crossed the road, and he didn't even wait for the light to change." At my husband's words, I looked up sharply.

"Caught you napping," Steve said, laughing.

I was trying hard to stay awake during our late Friday night trip to the Blue Heron Farm. It was a long ride, and the rural back roads were dark and remote.

Steve put his hand gently on mine. "Go back to sleep. I'll be fine. I can drive and watch for Martians at the same time." I barely heard his words as I fell back to sleep.

* * * * * *

42

I was awakened by a vivid bolt of lightning that opened the entire sky. Then the road was black again. Why was I so uneasy? I'd seen lightning before, and country roads are always dark.

As soon as we came to the familiar fork in the road, I felt more comfortable. But I could not shake the feeling that something was wrong.

I turned around to wake my two children and found Sharon and Jonathan staring intently out the window of the station wagon. That was certainly a surprise. How often does a ten-year-old boy sit quietly with his twelve-year-old sister?

Suddenly Jonathan spotted the stone wall that marks the boundary of the Blue Heron. We craned our necks for our first glimpse of the farm.

As we pulled into the dirt entrance road, I saw that the house was in total darkness. Charlie, the collie, came running out to meet us. He was whining strangely. Behind him, Arthur and Cindy appeared. They were yelling, "Don't turn it off! Don't turn it off!"

"Turn what off?" Steve asked, as he shut off the engine.

"Oh, no!" Cindy wailed. "You shouldn't have done that! We tried to call! You shouldn't have come! The telephone doesn't work! The car won't start! We're trapped here! We're trapped!"

At Arthur's insistence Steve tried to start the car. Again and again, he turned the key. There wasn't a sound from the engine.

"This isn't possible," I said, turning toward Cindy in amazement.

"What's going on, Arthur?" Steve asked.

"Come inside. We'll talk in the house."

Following the beam of Arthur's flashlight, we walked in silence to the farmhouse. We had no idea what had happened, but we could almost smell the danger.

As Cindy lit the candles, Arthur made sure all the windows were covered. Then he turned to us, saying, "It's like a nightmare."

"You tell it," Cindy said, her face twitching with fear.

"We were feeding and bedding down the livestock," Arthur told us. "It was quite dark because we were behind schedule tonight. The animals were restless. We figured a storm was approaching.

"As soon as we were back in the house, Cindy tried to get a weather report, but the radio would not work. Suddenly the lights went out. My first thought was that the storm had drawn near and lightning had struck a power line. I heard the livestock getting louder and louder. Suddenly I heard a deafening roar and saw a vivid bolt of lightning that seemed to open the entire sky."

I shivered at Arthur's words.

Arthur continued: "As I stepped out onto the porch, I saw the barn door fly open. I went inside the house, grabbed my rifle, and ran outside. I saw my animals all running. Cows, horses, pigs, goats, sheep—even the fowl—were all moving in one direction. They seemed to be moving against their will, as if drawn by some invisible force.

"Then I saw my horse, Gregor. I whistled to him. He always comes to my whistle. I saw him try to

turn, but he couldn't. Instead, he continued to move forward. I whistled again and again without any result.

"I turned just in time to grab Charlie, who was about to join the stream of livestock. I locked him in the house and went back out to follow the animals.

They were heading toward the alfalfa field.

"Then came a piercing noise. My head was ringing from the sound. My ears felt as if they would burst. I could go no further. Holding my ears, I ran, half-crazed, back toward the house.

"Cindy was in the car. She was behind the wheel crying, 'It won't start! It won't start!' I tried it myself but the engine was dead.

"We ran back to the house and locked ourselves in. When we remembered that you were coming, we tried to call you, but the telephone wouldn't work. Nothing mechanical works—not since the lights went out. We sat here for what seemed like hours. Then we heard your car coming up the road. You know the rest."

When Arthur stopped speaking, we sat staring at each other. My daughter was crying softly and clasping her father's hand.

"What do you think is going on?" my husband asked finally.

"It's as if some alien force has. . ." Arthur was cut off by a piercing noise, more painful than any I had ever heard before. It grew louder within seconds. All we could think of was running. Arthur grabbed the flashlight and lifted a trapdoor in the kitchen floor.

We climbed down the steps and groped our way to an old root cellar. Its thick stone walls blocked much of the tormenting noise. I clasped the children to me and sank down.

* * * * * *

After some hours, the noise stopped and we finally found the courage to leave the root cellar. Outside, it was quiet and bright like any other morning. It looked so normal that the previous hours seemed like a dream. But the farm was still deserted of livestock and nothing mechanical worked.

We walked around the farm and came upon two sheep grazing. That convinced Arthur that his horse was still on the farm. He suggested to Steve that they find the horse and hitch him to a wagon so we could leave.

"No way are you going to leave us alone," Cindy said. "We'll all go looking for Gregor."

Cautiously, we headed toward the alfalfa field, which had been harvested the previous week. Charlie, the collie, followed us.

"Look at the wheat field!" Sharon shouted. We all ran over to look at the next field, which we had helped cultivate and reap. We stared in amazement.

We saw a gigantic circle in the earth, as if the field had been stamped by a hot branding iron. Steam was still rising from the blackened earth. The circle was the size of a football field. Nervously, we began to walk around the circle and tried to imagine what could have caused it.

Suddenly Charlie barked and, with a weird whine, took off across the gully. Without thinking, my son, Jonathan, ran after the dog. Terrified of what might be out there, we yelled at him to stop, but Jonathan didn't hear us. I started after Jonathan and the others followed. I could see Jonathan's red jacket bobbing through the rows of Indian corn on the hill above. Without pausing for breath I ran through the rows of corn.

Jonathan stopped at the top of the hill and stood with his back to me. I reached my son, grabbed him, and turned him to me in relief as the others caught up. Then I saw Jonathan's eyes. They were still fixed in a wide stare. I turned to see what had captured his attention.

All of us gasped. We saw the object that had branded the circle on the wheat field. It looked like a flying saucer straight out of a comic book. Even in daylight, the craft was glowing with the cold light of a star at night. We had no doubt that this was an alien spaceship.

Hundreds of people were moving silently toward the ship as though drawn against their will. The aliens must have spotted us, for the tormenting noise of the night before returned. It was even more high-pitched and piercing.

"I'm scared, Mommy! Get me out of here! Don't let them take me!" Jonathan screamed. I clasped my son's arm.

We tried to resist the pull of the noise, but our feet slowly dragged us ever closer to the spaceship. Terror-stricken, I watched as my husband and daughter boarded the ship. I suddenly grew dizzy and weak. I felt my son slip out of my grasp just before I fainted.

When I came to, I was alone on the farm. The spaceship was gone. The animals were gone. My family and friends were gone.

Desperate to get help, I walked to the village. It, too, was deserted of all life. I returned to the farm.

Unable to bear the thought of never again seeing my husband and children, I await the aliens' return. They'll come again. I'm sure of it. They must ...they must!

by Arthur Myers

Do phantoms like to have their picture taken? Sometimes.

On page 4 of the August 24, 1978, *St. Paul Dispatch* are photographs of four faces. One photograph is of an old man with a long, white beard. Another is of a man with dark hair and a full, black beard. The third is of a young man with short chin whiskers, and the fourth is of a smiling young woman. The pictures are not sharp, but they would be recognized by anyone who knew the people.

What's unusual about these photographs is that the people weren't around when the pictures were taken. According to the photographer, these people have been dead for periods ranging from a few dozen to 2,000 years.

The photographer was a St. Paul, Minnesota, meatcutter named Gerry Gross, a quite ordinary man except for one thing. Gross claims he can see his guides—or, as they are called in some churches, guardian angels. The people in these pictures, he says, are his guides.

According to Gross, they appear to him often, and one day they suggested he take their pictures. He did, using his Polaroid camera, and the photographs resulted. However, Gross complains that his camera was ruined—the lens became fogged. The same thing happened when he later tried to use his movie camera on his guides. And this time they didn't even show up in the pictures.

Whether or not one believes Gross's account, taking photographs of ghosts is nothing new. It goes back more than 100 years, almost to the beginning of photography. That is, of course, if one accepts the very idea of spirit photography. On the one hand, so-called spirit photographers have been checked out by so-called experts for the last 100 years, and many have received clean bills of health. On the other hand, many of the photographers were judged to be quite "sick"—in other words, sheer cheats.

One of the best-known spirit photographers and one of the best-known doubting detectives both figured in a case that goes back to the early part of this century. The detective was none other than the famous magician, Houdini. Houdini took delight in exposing those who he felt were trying to kid the public. He seemed to feel they were trespassing on his private preserves. The man whose work he examined was Alexander Martin, a commercial photographer who had a studio in Denver, Colorado.

Martin took his first spirit pictures in 1879. He was taking tintypes of babies, and faces of children who were not visibly present appeared in the photographs. Sometimes he would take photographs of families, and "extras" would appear. These were usually the family's relatives or friends who had died.

Before Houdini came on the scene, Martin had been checked out by another famous fan of spirit activities, Sir Arthur Conan Doyle.

Doyle had been a doctor of medicine before he became a writer. It could therefore be argued that he was a man with a scientific approach to matters. Furthermore, Doyle gained fame as the inventor of Sherlock Holmes, the greatest detective of all time. If one wouldn't believe Doyle, whom would one believe? After investigating Martin, Doyle praised him as "one of the great spirit photographers of the world." Nonetheless, Houdini decided to take a look for himself.

In 1915, Houdini made a trip to Denver to determine if there was anything to Martin's by then famous pictures of phantoms. Martin took many photographs under Houdini's direction. Some were of Houdini himself. And some of the photographs, including at least one with Houdini in it, had "extras." Houdini watched Martin carefully at all stages of the loading, developing, and printing of the film. Afterward, the great master of tricks said, "I am perfectly convinced that he has the ability to capture the spirit world on film. I believe Alexander Martin to be honest and his craft authentic."

Of course, no one knows when the first spirit popped onto some startled photographer's film or plate. But the first person to advertise the notion that he could take such weird pictures was William Mumler of Boston. One day Mumler tried to take a photograph of himself by training the camera on an empty chair and jumping into position after taking the cap off the lens. When Mumler developed the plates, he discovered the figure of a young woman sitting on the chair. Her legs were transparent, fading off into a dim mist. Mumler said he recognized the girl as a cousin who had died twelve years before.

Soon Mumler set himself up as a commercial spirit photographer. He had abundant success until it was pointed out that some of the "extras" in his pictures were people who were still alive. Mumler left Boston for New York and set up shop. After a time, he was arrested for cheating the public. Mumler was brought to trial but was found not guilty when other photographers backed his story.

The fact that a living person appears in a spirit photograph need not mean that the picture should be condemned as a fake. A photograph of the government council hangs in the parliament building at Victoria, British Columbia. It was taken in 1865. One member of the council—Charles Good— was very ill, reported to be dying, and was not present when the picture was taken. Yet when the picture was developed, his face appeared with the four other members of the council.

And perhaps one should also not totally rule out the possibility of spirit photography because a photographer has been found to cheat in a particular situation. Humans are strange. Sometimes people who have deservedly gained a reputation for honesty will suddenly cheat. They have, in a way, become victims of their talents. Spirit photographers feel they have to live up to their reputations by producing a spirit in every photograph. Unfortunately, the spirits don't always agree, and the photographers may then cheat.

The first English spirit photographer was Frederick Hudson. He became known for many spirit photographs taken under careful test conditions and judged to be true pictures of phantoms. Yet he was also caught cheating from time to time.

Another in-and-out, yes-and-then-again-no spirit photographer was an Englishman named John Myers. Myers, a former dentist, produced photographs of some famous people who had died. Many experts felt that Myers was honest much of the time. But there was some question as to just *when*. One doubter, the Marquess of Donegall, carried out a careful test on Myers. Lord Donegall loaded the camera and developed the film himself. A leading magician watched closely. Six photographs were taken in bright light while Myers simply stood by. Two of the pictures showed figures of men who could not be accounted for. Lord Donegall announced his satisfaction with Myers in an article in the *Sunday Dispatch* in 1932. However, a week later, following another sitting, Donegall accused Myers of switching plates.

Some years ago, the writer of this article was the editor of a magazine in New England. One year I was looking for a good cover picture for Halloween. By chance I ran across a perfect photograph in another magazine and made arrangements to use it. It showed four foggy phantoms floating across a cemetery. It seemed too good to be true. But after the magazine came out, I became so curious about the weird picture that I looked up the photographer.

Her name was Ethel Whitaker, and she lived in Monroe, Connecticut. She was a schoolteacher who worked with children who had learning problems. She and her husband had moved to Connecticut in 1958, and one day she decided to take a picture of him standing in the drive of their new home. When the film was printed, it also showed two children—a boy and a girl—in the drive. The girl was standing; the boy was sitting on a bicycle. The children were dressed in clothing of the 1920s.

Mrs. Whitaker's husband insisted that she must have made some technical mistake in loading the film or using the camera. Mrs. Whitaker wasn't so sure he was right. She put the picture in the family album with other, less strange ones.

Some years later, Mrs. Whitaker heard a radio interview with a married couple who had gained a reputation as experts in spirit communication. They lived not far away. She went to them and showed them the odd photograph, as well as others she had some questions about. They said she was a true spirit photographer, and invited her to go with them on their expeditions to haunted houses.

Since then, Mrs. Whitaker has taken photographs of many ghosts, ranging from an old sea captain to a group of nuns. She says she has no idea how she does it. She says she can't see anything. She just snaps the shutter, and the pictures of phantoms show up on the film.

Do the pictures really show spirits? The answer depends on what you believe. But if you have a camera and are curious to know whether a spirit is hovering around you, try taking a picture.

If books can't be judged by their covers, can presidential candidates be judged by their biographies?

The Way to Become President

by Arthur Myers

One of the time-honored customs of United States presidential politics is the writing of a campaign biography of the candidate.

True, the first ten men who ran for the nation's highest office made it without such help. But then in 1828, Andrew Jackson was swept into office. Everyone noted that a book listing his accomplishments and telling his life story in the most complimentary terms had been widely read by the voters.

The lesson was not lost on those who practice the political arts. Since that time, candidates who have managed to get their names on the presidential ballot have never failed to have a book written about them. On occasion, they have even gone to the lengths of writing that book themselves, witness Jimmy Carter's modestly titled book, *Why Not the Best?*

Humbleness, carefully mixed with pride of accomplishment, is considered the magic key to political success. Nothing, at least according to political wisdom, can beat a person whom voters see as being smarter than themselves—but not too much smarter. The candidate can be capable, honest, reasonably intelligent, maybe even cultivated, but underneath it all he or she must come over unmistakably as "just one of the people."

Take for example Henry Clay, who ran against Andrew Jackson in 1832. The forgotten writer of Clay's campaign biography showed that he had studied Jackson's 1828 campaign biography. Of course, Clay had quite a record of accomplishments, which had to be played up—but then again, down. Here is an example of the way Clay's writer went about the job:

"Much as we admire Henry Clay the public speaker, Henry Clay the commanding Speaker of the House of Representatives, Henry Clay the Minister, Henry Clay the Secretary of State, Henry Clay the grave and able Senator, Henry Clay the favorite of the people, yet do we love far more to consider the orphan boy, following the plow in the slashes of Hanover, and occasionally trudging his way with a sack of corn to a distant mill, to provide bread for a widowed mother and younger brothers and sisters."

One can imagine the writer of that amazing sentence laying down his pen and sighing in satisfaction, "That ought to do it!" It didn't: Jackson won again.

Having a widowed mother was important in politics of those days, but not as important as being born in a log cabin. If a presidential candidate hadn't been born in a log cabin, it helped if he at least had spent time in or around some sort of log structure.

The log-cabin issue seems to have taken hold during the successful 1840 campaign of William Henry "Tippecanoe and Tyler Too" Harrison. He won an avalanche of votes as the "log-cabin candidate."

Daniel Webster was so upset by this gap in his own personal history that he whined publicly, "It did not happen to me to be born in a log cabin, but my older brothers and sisters were born in a log cabin and raised among the snowdrifts of New Hampshire." On top of failing to be born in a building made of logs, Webster also had a mother who was not widowed. Webster never made it beyond the Senate.

The man who wrote Horace Greeley's campaign biography tried desperately to get around his candidate's problem. He admitted that Greeley had not been born in a log cabin, but made it clear that Greeley's birthplace was "small and unpainted." The writer also suggested that the school Greeley had attended was built of logs. It was a nice try, but it didn't work.

Rutherford B. Hayes, 19th President of the United States, had better luck. Though his birthplace was made of brick, his parents fortunately had added a wing made of logs.

Campaign biographers concentrate on many ways to influence the voters. They discourage any suggestion that their candidate is in the slightest degree high and mighty. Take, for example, Horatio Seymour, who ran against Ulysses S. Grant in 1868. Seymour had gone to college, not a common experience in those days. His biographer tried to get around this problem by skipping Seymour's school days altogether. He brought his hero to the age of 31 in two pages of a 292-page book.

On the other hand, Al Smith was a natural. He was one of the greatest vote-getters of all time. When Smith ran for the Presidency in 1928, he was praised for having attended the "University of Hard Knocks." He was the proud owner, his writer observed, of a "clear mind unburdened by mere vocabularly" and other such useless baggage. Smith lost nonetheless—though not by much—to Herbert Hoover.

Although the candidates can't seem high and mighty, they have to stand out in some way. After all, they're running for the highest office in the land. Long ago, campaign writers determined that the candidate should be better in some way that is not threatening to the voting public. For example, it was maintained that, when a boy, Cal Coolidge could get more syrup out of maple trees than the other children could. It's hard to get jealous over that sort of thing. And Zachary Taylor was a fine fellow to have around during an Indian attack. (Come to think of it, so was the actor John Wayne. If Wayne had run for President, he probably would have won.) Horace Greeley, it was said, could read adult books "right-side-up, upside down, or sidewise" at the age of four. This, however, was dangerous because it suggested real talent. Anyone planning to write a campaign biography should note that Coolidge and Taylor were elected, Greeley wasn't.

A campaign biographer is better advised to stress lack of talent. In this regard, the biographer of

Warren Harding had it made, and he took full advantage of his opportunities. One of the best examples of the just-one-of-the-regular-people school of writing appears in Harding's biography: "The child grew up as he should—to be just a boy, not a prodigy, but humanly normal."

Thomas E. Dewey had a hard row to hoe, for he was running against Franklin D. Roosevelt during World War II. His biographer rose nobly to the occasion, particularly in his use of the just-an-average-fellow approach. He pointed out that Dewey stood a bit short for a public man. But at five feet eight inches (1.7 meters), Dewey was almost exactly the height of the average man in the armed forces. That non-accomplishment wasn't enough for Dewey to beat Roosevelt.

Writers often have to think very hard to come up with something interesting about their subjects. McKinley's writer met the challenge by pointing out that his candidate's shoes were always shined, and that he shaved very closely without ever cutting himself. The high point of the book might well be the mention that McKinley could "carry on a conversation while cutting off his beard."

In the past, the "odd happening" was also heavily relied on. William Henry Harrison was praised for having taken part in the Indian wars upon reaching the same age at which Lafayette had joined the American Revolution. Coolidge, it was pointed out, had many of the same experiences as previous honored holders of the presidential office. Like Lincoln, Coolidge had been brought up by a step-mother. Like Cleveland and Wilson, he had dropped his first name and used his middle name. Furthermore, he was born on the Fourth of July, and was elected to the office of Vice President when he was 48—one year for each star of the flag in use at that time. When Coolidge ran for President, in 1924, he was 52, the same age as Abraham Lincoln when Lincoln became President. How could he lose?

If no ties to the past are conveniently available, the writer can always grope around for an interesting first or two. And so, the voters were told that Harding, if elected, would be the first son of a Civil War soldier to become President. Not only that, he would be the first President to have a father still leading an active business life. In spite of not having a widowed mother, Harding won.

Most of the people who write campaign biographies are little-known writers, often newspaper reporters out to make a quick buck. But some famous writers have also had a go at it. Nathaniel Hawthorne wrote the life of his old college friend, Franklin Pierce. President Pierce rewarded Hawthorne by making him consul in Liverpool. William Dean Howells wrote a book about Lincoln without putting himself to the bother of visiting his subject. For this work, Howells received an appointment as consul in Venice. Lew Wallace, Governor of New Mexico Territory from 1878 to 1881 and writer of the book *Ben Hur*, turned his hand to a campaign biography on Benjamin Harrison.

The torchlight parade and the stump speech of the old-time campaigns have faded into the mists of time. But to this day, in spite of television, the campaign biography marches crazily on.

Football player Roy Riegels had an unfortunate date with fame at...

The Rose Bowl of 1929

by Arthur Myers

Half a century ago, most famous football players were amateurs, usually playing on high school or college teams. They didn't get paid to play. They played for fun—and for applause. They actually thought football was a game!

Today, most of the famous athletes are the professionals. But in those days before World War II, the college players were the national idols. And the high point of the football season was the Rose Bowl game in Pasadena, California, played on New Year's Day. On that day, few Americans were out of range of the radio broadcast of the big game.

In the Rose Bowl, the best college football team in the East meets the best team in the West. That, at least, is the theory, although each year a few million fans are bound to disagree with the officials who pick the teams. For example, in 1929 almost everyone agreed that Georgia Tech was the champion of the East, but there was some question about the University of California, which represented the West.

The University of California had not had a fabulous football season. Its team had won six games, lost two, and tied one. It was, in fact, second choice. The University of Southern California had been asked first but had refused after a dispute with the Tournament of Roses officials.

Still, the University of California team was believed to have a good chance. After all, anything can happen in a football game. In fact, the betting odds favored California slightly—but perhaps only because West Coast sportswriters had established the odds.

And so, on the first day of 1929, about 72,000 people packed into the Rose Bowl. Most were from the West Coast, hoping for a pleasant surprise. They were surprised, all right, but not the way they expected.

From the very beginning of the game, the California boys seemed determined to disappoint the hometown fans, although they had some help from the referee. First, the California tailback, Benny Lom, threw a pass to a receiver standing alone in the end zone. The receiver dropped the ball. Then Lom, who was voted Player of the Day after the game, scooped up a Georgia fumble and raced 60 yards (55 meters) for a touchdown. Only it wasn't a touchdown. The referee had blown the play dead before Lom had started running. Later the official admitted it was a "quick whistle"—a mistake.

And so, nearing the end of the first half, instead of California being two touchdowns ahead, the game was a scoreless tie. And then history took a quick but lasting glance at a young man named Roy Riegels.

Riegels was a blond, blue-eyed junior who played center for California. He was of average size for a college player of the time. He stood 6 feet (1.8 meters) and weighed 170 pounds (63 kilograms). To play in the line of a major college football team, let alone on a professional team, today, a man would have to weigh about 100 pounds (36 kilograms) more than Riegels did.

Riegels stood out in his accomplishments on the field. He had been picked as an All-Coast lineman after the University of California team had completed its regulation schedule. In two full years of college football, he had missed only four minutes of action. Injury seemed to be something that happened to other players, not to Riegels. He was no backfield flash like Benny Lom, who caught the public's eye, but the other team always knew Riegels was there. He was a calm, mature young man who made few mistakes. To his teammates, Riegels was a star. As they went into the Rose Bowl game, Riegels was considered to be the most likely candidate for the next team captain.

With the first half drawing to a close, Georgia Tech had the ball in its own territory. The Eastern team's most dangerous outside runner, Stumpy Thomason, took a pitch from his quarterback and raced for 15 yards (14 meters). California end Irv Phillips hit him with a jarring tackle, and the ball popped loose. It bounced around crazily, looking for a taker. It was Roy Riegels' date with fame.

A lineman rarely gets to touch the football. When he does, all bets are off. With a ball in his hands, a lineman is out of his depth. Often he is so surprised to find himself the center of the entire arena's attention that he tenses up and does weird things. Sometimes he trips himself up before anyone else can do it for him. Or he stands stock still in obvious fright until an opposing player knocks him down and puts him out of his distress. Then he lies still, covering the ball like a mother hen, grateful for the familiar feeling of trampling feet on his back.

Had Roy Riegels taken one of these courses, his name would never have gone down in the history of American sports. But Riegels did not freeze like a normal lineman, nor did he trip. He was fast for a lineman to begin with. Perhaps he harbored some secret trace of bitterness at the applause that was the lot of the fleet backfield men, the ball carriers—particularly since he himself could run as fast as many of them. At any rate, Roy Riegels decided that his moment of glory had been thrust upon him. He grabbed the loose ball on the bounce and started running.

There was nothing but daylight between him and the goalposts. He could see the five-yard (4.5-meter) stripes flashing under his feet. The goal loomed nearer and nearer. The crowd roared. No one

seemed near him. Except, wait...

Riegels could hear a pounding behind him. Closer and closer it came. Then he heard a voice yelling, "Stop, stop!"

How odd, Riegels thought, that a Georgia Tech

player should shout at him to stop. What a strange way to try to influence an opposing player in a football game. Had it ever worked? Curious, Riegels shot a glance back over his shoulder. To his surprise the player chasing him was not from Georgia Tech. The pursuer was none other than his friend and teammate, Benny Lom, one of the fastest men in football. Only he could have caught up with the flying Riegels. A quick glance told Riegels that the rest of the California team was also pounding along not far behind Lom.

And where was Georgia Tech? Standing about open-eyed, back in the general area where Riegels had originally picked up the ball.

Then Riegels could hear Lom more clearly. "Stop, stop, you're going the wrong way!" Lom was shouting. It must have been one of the great "Oops, sorries" in the history of sports.

Riegels stopped short, on the California one-yard line. Lom grasped Riegels' arm and tried to turn him around in the other direction. But Georgia Tech had come to life and joined the party. They smothered Riegels before he had a chance to go more than a step or two back up the field.

It was California's ball on its own one-yard line, the worst possible position to be in. Lom tried to kick out from behind the goal line, but the kick was blocked. Because the ball landed behind the Georgia Tech goalpost, Georgia Tech was awarded two points. As it turned out, this was the victory edge for the Eastern team. Both teams scored touchdowns in the second half, and the game ended 9-7 in Georgia Tech's favor.

Riegels felt worse about the mistake than anyone else. He tried to leave the game for a substitute, but the coach wouldn't let him. After the game, his team-mates gave him a huge vote of confidence by electing him captain for the coming year. In his last year of college, Riegels again made All-Coast center.

But the public didn't forget. Throughout his life, Riegels has been known as "Wrong-Way Riegels." He spent the early part of his life as a high school football coach. Later he founded Roy Riegels Chemicals, a fertilizer business, in the town of Woodland in northern California. He spends much of his time visiting farmers. But even out among the rye and alfalfa, he can't escape the slight slip he made that first day of 1929. Riegels has always had an easy-going personality. But sometimes he gets tired of people, when they first meet him, saying, "Riegels? Not Wrong-Way Riegels!" And sometimes their laughter is not good-natured.

"I've never hit anyone," Riegels says, "but there have been times I wanted to kick some people in the rear end."

Benny Lom tells a story about that famous day. About fifteen years later, Riegels and he were having a drink at Lom's house. Lom played a record of the radio broadcast of Riegels' run in the wrong direction.

"Then," Lom says, "Roy looked at me and con-fessed, 'Benny, remember when you grabbed my arm at their goal line? I thought you wanted me to give you the ball so you could score the touchdown.' "

Both men laughed. After fifteen years, it seemed funny.

If two runners are about equal, it all comes down to what's going on in their minds.

The Sixth Hurdle

Part 1
by Daniel J. Domoff

Noah Wright, my sometimes friend, was whisper-
ing at me from the end of the lockers: "Hey, Speed. I
heard that Quentin ran the 110-meter hurdles in
fourteen seconds flat in practice Tuesday. Fourteen
flat. What do you say about that?"

I never can tell if Noah is trying to discourage me or spur me on. Or if he is just jealous. That's why I call him my "sometimes friend."

"Stuff it, Noah," I said. "I don't need to hear that right now." I was taping my sore ankle. I had knocked down a hurdle in practice and had a neat little bump on the inside right anklebone.

A week from Saturday, there is going to be the biggest track meet of the season. The best athletes from three states will be there. Noah was talking about Maurice Quentin, a hurdler from Devoy. Quentin is one of the two best schoolboy hurdlers in the area. Maybe in the whole country. One of the two best. I'm the other one.

My name is Richard Carr. My friends call me "Speed" because I'm so fast. Put my nickname together with my last name and you've got "Speed Carr." Sounds like a ride at an amusement park. It's a good name for a hurdler.

Fourteen flat, I thought to myself. That's fast. Too fast for a high school kid. I don't believe it.

My race is the 110-meter hurdles. It's a tough event. You need speed, but that's not all. Your form has to be perfect. Perfect steps, right over all ten hurdles. Barely clearing them. If you're too high, you're wasting time in the air. If you're too low, you crash the hurdle and lose even more time. And maybe hurt yourself. Like I did today in practice.

Fourteen flat, I thought again. Heck, maybe Quentin did do it, but it's hard to believe. Fourteen flat would have won the Olympics 50 years ago. My best is 14.3 seconds. I think Quentin's just trying to scare me. So he sent out the word he ran a fourteen flat. I don't believe it.

If two runners are about equal, it all comes down to what's going on in their minds. It's a form of combat, like boxing. Who can scare whom? Who has more confidence? The one who feels sharper will be quicker off the starting blocks. The one who's concentrating more will have better form going over the hurdles. But if you're too tense, you lose.

I always go over the first five hurdles beautifully. Then for a split second, I lose concentration. The sixth hurdle is on me before I know it. My leading leg, the left one, goes over a bit high. I try to correct myself, but I bring my trailing leg over a bit low. Crack. That's why I have a bandage on my right ankle now.

Besides Quentin, no other hurdler around here can catch me, even if I knock over the sixth hurdle. I'm too far ahead by then. I get my form back together for the last four hurdles and then breeze to the tape. No one's near me. But if I crash a hurdle when running against Maurice Quentin, forget it. He's gone. His heels will be in my face, his dust in my throat.

I have a little over a week for my ankle to get better. But in the meanwhile, I have to keep practicing. I have to work on my form, especially over that sixth hurdle. The coach will help me. But it's hard to practice when you have any kind of injury. I'm just going to have to work on getting stronger. And I'll try not to worry about Maurice Quentin. Even if he *did* run a fourteen flat.

Ooo. My ankle hurts.

Noah was still sitting down at the end of the

lockers.

"Hey, Noah," I said. "You tell Quentin that *I* ran a fourteen flat in practice today. Got that? Fourteen seconds flat. In a sweatsuit! You hear? And in sneakers. No spikes—sneakers! And with a bum ankle!"

Noah just smiled. "Heck, Speed, I couldn't say any of that. I don't tell lies. And all that would be a lie—except for the part about the bum ankle."

Noah showed his own speed when one of my spiked shoes came flying at his head.

I dressed slowly. I knew I couldn't think about Maurice Quentin too much. That would be my doom. If I concentrated only on my own speed and form, then the race against Quentin would take care of itself. Sure, I want to win. More than anything. But it won't be the end of the world if I lose. I just want to do my best. That way, if I lose, it will be an honorable loss.

Of course, if I win, it would be only a minor accomplishment. It would give me only as much satisfaction, say, as being elected President of the country. Something small like that.

But that Noah Wright bugs me. What is it about his personality that makes him needle me so much? It's as if he's always itching to start a dispute with me. I never did anything bad to him. He acts like a friend for a while, and then he goes on a campaign to make me angry. I can't figure it.

I walked slowly out of the locker room, down the hallway, and out of the school. The street was quiet. All the other kids had gone home long before. My ankle still hurt, and it's a long walk home, so I decided to take the bus. While waiting at the bus stop, I loosened my shoe to take some of the pressure off my ankle.

Just then, Noah wandered over. "Hey, Speed. How's the ankle? Want me to call an ambulance?"

I glared at him. "You're the one who's going to need the ambulance if you don't shut up."

"My, my," Noah said. "Have you got a short fuse! Hey, relax, Speed. We're pals, remember?"

"Sometimes I wonder."

"Wonder what?"

"If we're really pals, Noah. You keep riding me. I mean, you almost seem happy I cracked my ankle today. If we're such pals, you ought to give me a boost now and then. Instead, you ride me."

"Whoa—now wait a minute, Speed. I admit, maybe sometimes it's hard for me to resist kidding you. But there's no one, I repeat, *no one*, who wants you to beat Quentin as much as I do." Noah placed his right hand over his left and put them both on his chest. "Cross my heart."

"Sure, sure," I said, and looked down the street for the bus.

"Well," Noah started to speak, but then stopped. He looked down at the ground, staring at a spot. I looked over and realized he was watching a tiny ant crawl along the sidewalk. He was just about to step on it, but he stopped. Unaware of how close it had just come to being crushed, the ant reached a few blades of grass that stuck out of a crack in the sidewalk. It struggled to get over them. Courageous in its effort, the little insect succeeded.

"Speed," Noah looked up thoughtfully, "I know I'll

never be the runner you are. But that doesn't matter. I want to see you win. It won't be easy for you to beat Quentin. But I think you can do it. I mean—I know you can. If I ride you a little, it's only because I want you to loosen up. You're too tense. If you go into that race too tense. . . ."

"I know," I said, "I'll lose."

"That's right."

"Well, listen, Noah. Your telling me that Quentin ran a fourteen flat isn't exactly helping me relax. You know what I mean?"

"Hey—I'm sorry about that."

I turned and looked up the block again. The bus was coming. "You don't take this bus, do you?" I asked Noah.

"No. I can walk home."

"Okay," I said. "I'll see you."

"Speed," Noah said. "One more thing."

"What's that?"

"Quentin didn't run a fourteen flat in practice. I was just kidding."

I smiled. The bus came and I got on. I felt as if I had reached an armistice of some sort with Noah. I sat down by an open window and looked at Noah out on the sidewalk. He was watching the ant again.

Just before the bus pulled away, Noah looked up at me. Then suddenly he shouted, and his voice invaded the whole bus. "Quentin didn't run a four-teen flat! He ran a thirteen-nine!" I laughed out loud as Noah Wright, my full-time friend, raced off down the block.

End of Part I

76

A hurdle is a hurdle. Or is it?

The Sixth Hurdle

Part 2
by Daniel J. Domoff

The sky was high and bright. I lay back on the grass in the infield of the track and lazily watched the thin white clouds evaporate in the warm morning air. It was peaceful. In a grove of trees on the other side of the track, a bird sprang into song. Lightly, I dozed. With the earth at my back and the sun above me, I felt surrounded by great forces of growth and heat. Energy flowed into my body. I felt strong.

It was Saturday. In one week I would step out onto a track in another state. I would stand shoulder to shoulder with five other young men at the starting line of the 110-meter hurdle race. We would be called to our marks. We would crouch at the line, our feet in the starting blocks. Five other young men, but I feared only one of them: Maurice Quentin. The only one who could beat me. The only one who could beat me was...

"Richard."

"Come on, Speed, wake up."

"Richard!"

My eyes opened. Standing there above me were Coach Thorp and my friend, Noah Wright.

"That's how you train, Speed?" Noah said. "Flat on your back?"

"You must be extremely confident, Richard," said the coach. "Come on, get up. We have work to do."

I got to my feet as Noah got down to the ground to do push-ups.

"How's the injury?" the coach asked. I had knocked my ankle on the sixth hurdle the previous Thursday.

"Okay," I said. "Hurts a little."

"A little?" the coach said. "Let me see it."

"It's taped," I said.

"Let me see it!" the coach repeated, a bit urgently.

I raised the leg on my sweat pants and the coach knelt to investigate. "I don't see any swelling," he said.

"It's gone down."

"Good. You'll live. Have you warmed up at all?"

"A little," I lied.

"A little?" said the coach. "A little? Well, get yourself loose. Then jog eight laps. You too, Noah."

". . . forty-nine, fifty," Noah said, as he finished his push-ups.

As the coach walked away, Noah sat and looked at me. "You should retire from track, Speed. Take up soccer."

"Sure," I grinned at him as I started stretching. "Does Maurice Quentin play soccer?"

"I thought you weren't going to think about Quentin," Noah said, serious for the moment.

I said nothing. In my mind, I saw Quentin, the only one who could beat me. He had long legs, long hurdler's legs. Longer than mine. He was scientific in the way he went about hurdling, carefully studying every part of the race. And Quentin was so explosive over those hurdles. As if he were shot from a gun.

The only one who could beat me.

"Speed," Noah said quietly, "don't beat yourself."

"What do you mean?" I asked.

"Don't beat yourself," he repeated. And that was all.

We finished stretching and started to jog. Other athletes were beginning to arrive at the track. They said "Hi" as Noah and I ran past. We circled the track and reached the straightaway. The coach was setting up the hurdles for my practice. "Does the coach seem tense to you?" I asked Noah between breaths.

"Heck," said Noah, "tense is normal for the coach. If he weren't tense, he wouldn't be happy." And we ran the rest of the way in good spirits.

Finishing, we jogged over to the coach.

"Warmed up?" the coach asked. The sweat trickled along my brow and neck.

"A hundred percent warm," said Noah, "and ready to run, run, run."

"Good," said the coach. "Noah, you lead the others in ten fast sixties. I'm going to work with Mr. Richard 'Speed' Carr here."

"Check," said Noah, and he jogged away.

I watched the coach's eyes. He stared straight at me, holding my gaze. Then he spoke slowly. "Richard, in the race, all that matters are those hurdles. Ten hurdles. You have to get over them as smoothly and as quickly as you can. Fluid and smooth, like water in a stream. Quick, like a gray fox. Nothing else matters. The people you're running against don't matter. The stopwatch doesn't even matter. All that matters are the hurdles."

The coach had made this speech to me a hundred times. Even so, I couldn't help thinking about the people I would run against. And Quentin, the only one who could beat me.

"In the blocks," the coach commanded.

I crouched at the line, my feet in the blocks.

"I want you to take it easy the first time," said the coach. "Over the hurdles, good form, nice and easy."

He produced a small starter's pistol from his pocket. "On your mark."

I pressed my hands into the dirt just inside the line.

"No false starts, Richard. Don't jump the gun. Stay loose and ready."

The coach raised his gun. "Now set." I raised myself into the set position and stared ahead of me. The hurdles stood before me, one behind another, straight and stiff, like a row of dominoes.

POW! I was off.

* * * * * *

After practice, the coach spoke with me again. "Not bad, Richard. You were a bit high going over the hurdles. Probably worried about that ankle. But your form was good. You weren't leaning to the left. Your balance was good. I timed you once at 14.7 seconds. Not bad."

"The sixth hurdle bothers me, Coach. That's the one I always knock down."

"Every good hurdler has knocked down hurdles. A hurdle is a hurdle. You don't have time to count them as you're going over them. Why should the sixth bother you any more than the others?"

"I lose concentration there—halfway through the race."

"Richard, if you can't concentrate for fourteen seconds, then you have more problems than a few stupid hurdles." He put his hand on my shoulder. "Rest tomorrow. See you Monday."

"OK," I said.

"You'll do all right, Richard."

"Thanks, Coach."

* * * * * *

Monday, in chemistry class, the teacher dropped a piece of metal into a jar full of strong acid. The metal dissolved. I secretly envied that piece of metal. I too wanted to dissolve, fade away. Then I wouldn't have to face long-legged runners or dusty stretches of track filled with hurdles.

I remembered a dream I had had the night before. I was running the hurdles, but the track was like molasses. I was fighting just to move. I saw Maurice Quentin, but then suddenly he was gone. Had I passed him? I wasn't sure. Then I came up to the sixth hurdle. It was higher than the others, much higher. I could hardly see the top. How could I jump over it? Then I saw my friend Noah, and he was laughing: "Stay loose, Speed! Loose as a goose!" And I soared over the sixth hurdle as if I were born to fly.

After school, I practiced without taping my ankle. It felt fine. The coach timed me over the hurdles. He smiled, but he didn't tell me my time.

Tuesday, I didn't practice over hurdles. The coach wanted me to work on endurance. I ran slowly and steadily for an hour. Then I ran some wind sprints. Noah ran with me. I felt good.

Wednesday, I ran hurdles again. "Nothing else matters, Richard," the coach kept saying, "just the hurdles." I knocked over a couple of hurdles, but I was good and smooth over the sixth, and I never hurt my ankle.

On Thursday, the coach came over and sat down while I was loosening up. Noah was pushing on my back as I stretched toward my toes. The coach was quiet for a moment. He kind of looked off into the distance, watching a tree climb into the sky. "Today's the last practice before the meet. I want you to rest tomorrow."

I nodded.

"You give it everything you have. Today. Saturday. Always. When you do your best, try your hardest, no one can really beat you, even if others do better. As long as you do your best, you won't beat yourself. Now get warm. I want to time you."

The coach timed me three times, but he didn't speak to me until practice was over. "You did well today, Richard. Your form was excellent. You were fast..."

"I thought only of the hurdles, Coach."

"Your times were 14.2 seconds, 14.2 seconds again, and 14.1. You're ready. See you Saturday."

And two mornings later, I stood on a track in another state, shoulder to shoulder with five other young men, but I wasn't really aware of them. Among them stood one whose name I once had feared.

At the words "On your mark," I crouched at the line, my feet in the blocks. At the words "Now set," I leaned forward and up, staring ahead at the track. I saw nothing but my lane and the hurdles that stood within it. The warm sun beat down upon me, and I felt strong, strong enough to fly.

POW. The gun went off, and I soared.

Ira loves horror movies, but the monsters in his life
are real.

The Boy Who Lived With Monsters

by Cole Gagne

Well after midnight, Ira sat in his pajamas and watched TV. He felt sort of hungry, but didn't dare go downstairs to the kitchen. He stayed where he was, his face only inches away from the TV screen. On one of his good days, Ira's father had said that the distance from Ira's nose to the TV screen was so small, an ant with a bad back could jump it. But this was one of his bad days, and he would yell, not crack a joke, if he caught Ira up at night watching TV. Ira kept his door shut and the sound extremely low.

Ira's room was filled with all sorts of posters and photographs from monster movies. He didn't hang around the house very much anymore, so he enjoyed this chance to just look at them all by the dim light of the TV. That was only during the commercials, of course, because the movie tonight was one of Ira's favorites: *The Devil Bat*, with Bela Lugosi. In this one, Bela played a mad scientist who grew this gigantic bat. Whenever he wanted to kill people, Bela would splash a special shaving lotion on them. Then at night the bat would smell the scent, swoop down on them, and tear out their throats. "Go get 'em, bat!" Ira whispered to himself.

In the movie, Bela was just about to leave his next victim. "Good night," the doomed man cheerfully said. "Good-by," the cunning Bela replied, his voice oozing with monstrous anticipation. Ira said good-by along with Bela, carefully imitating the master's menacing tone. Ira had gotten the voices of both Boris Karloff and Bela Lugosi down pat by now; Vincent Price was still giving him a hard time, though. So during the commercial, as a lady talked on and on about how great her used cars were, Ira sat in his chair and repeated several times, "The pit...and...the PENDULUM," trying to recreate Price's enthusiastic voice.

Ira stopped when he heard his mother yelling at his father. He turned off the sound on the TV and listened. He wasn't really trying to catch her words, because he knew what she would be saying: she would be yelling at him for drinking too much. Ira knew that she yelled at his father only when she was drunk as well. Usually, Ira's mother got drunk only when his father was around. It didn't really surprise Ira to hear her yelling; she'd been doing that a lot these days.

Ira heard footsteps coming quickly up the stairs. He snapped off the TV and jumped into bed, lying there as if he had been asleep all night. Neither of his parents had ever gone into his room when they were like this, but who knows? Maybe this time one of them would. Ira relaxed when he heard a bedroom door slam shut: that would be his mother. Any moment now, he would hear—there it was: the sound of his father's car jerking out of the garage and weaving off into the night.

Knowing that his mother would stay in the bedroom until late the next afternoon, Ira went back to the TV. It was already near the end of the movie— they always cut the originals for TV. This was the part where the tables are turned, and a man splashes Bela with the special shaving lotion. Suddenly Ira was vividly reminded of the time his mother had thrown a drink in his father's face. But instead of slapping his attacker, as Ira's father had done, Bela shuddered with horror and ran off into the night, right into the waiting fangs of his own Devil Bat.

* * * * * *

The next day, Ira got together with Hal, a friend who was in Ira's sixth-grade class. They planned to play in the park for a while, and then go over to Hal's house to see *The Blob* on TV. *The Hideous Sun Demon* was playing at the same time on another channel, but Ira liked *The Blob* better. In that one, this meteor crashes on earth, and this weird, jellylike substance gets out and eats all these people, almost including Steve McQueen. Ira also looked forward to staying for dinner at Hal's. These days, he wound up eating there at least once a week. Hal's mother didn't seem to mind.

Ira and Hal had been in the park for only a little while when a bunch of tough kids from the junior high school came along. They saw Ira and Hal and slowly started to head in their direction. To Ira, they resembled the flesh-eating corpses of *Night of the Living Dead*, all lazily moving in for the kill. Ira turned to Hal, saying, "We'd better get going," but saw that Hal was already running off into the distance. Turning back, he saw that the older boys had suddenly begun running toward him. Ira started to run, but they caught up with him, and they shoved him around and laughed at him and took most of his money, and one kid pushed him into a muddy puddle.

As Ira headed for home, it began to rain. Pulling his jacket collar up around his neck, he started moving more quickly. He couldn't really run because he had hurt his leg when that kid pushed him down. When he reached home, Ira saw his father's car in the garage. He could hear his parents arguing in the living room. Not wanting to walk into that, and not wanting to stay out in the rain anymore, Ira went into the garage. It wasn't so bad: there was a towel there, so he could dry himself, and he could sit around in the beat-up old chair.

He poked around in the garage and found a box of old magazines. In it was an old issue of *Famous Monsters of Filmland* that Ira had been looking for for some time. He sat in the garage, flipping through the magazine, when all at once, much to his surprise, he began to cry. Ira hadn't cried over all this for at least a month. He thought he had finally gotten used to it all, that none of it could hurt him anymore. He suddenly became afraid that he would never get used to it, that it would always be there, pulling him down. This made him cry even more.

He stopped crying when he heard his father leave the house and head out to the garage. Ira could hear him muttering to himself and fumbling with his car keys. He could also hear his mother cursing at his father from the house. The chair Ira was sitting in was right near the door of the garage, but Ira decided to hide inside rather than run out and risk being stopped by his parents. So he jumped to the floor and scurried under the chair. It was a tight fit for a twelve-year-old, and he had squeezed only his head and chest under it when his father entered. His father got into the car from the side opposite Ira and didn't see his son's outstretched legs, so it really wasn't his fault when he backed the car out and drove over both of Ira's legs.

* * * * * *

Ira wound up lying in a bed in some hospital. Actually, he had been pretty lucky. A neighbor had heard his yelps of pain, gone out to investigate, and found him. The doctors said that what had happened to Ira wasn't really too bad, and they took X rays of his legs and put casts on them. He'd have to stay in bed for a while, then he'd be in a wheelchair for a while, and then he'd be on crutches for a while, but after that he'd be OK.

Ira had to share his room with some old man, but the man couldn't hear too well and slept most of the time, so Ira pretty much took over the TV set that was in their room. His second night in the hospital, Ira put on *Invasion of the Body Snatchers*. In this one, these giant seeds from outer space come to earth. Then whenever someone falls asleep, a seed opens. Out pops a being that looks just like the person who fell asleep, and the real person disappears. Someone you thought you knew would turn out to be this monster from another planet.

Ira watched the scene where the young boy was trying to convince Kevin McCarthy that his mother was no longer his mother. McCarthy didn't believe him. Ira, having seen the film more than once, smiled to himself. Just you wait, smart guy, he thought happily. In less than two hours you'll wind up running out onto a highway, struggling hopelessly to stop a car, any car, desperate to get someone to listen to you, to know what you've learned: "You're in danger! They're here already! You're next! You're next!"

Jan de Hartog wrote adventure stories and lived them too.

The Adventures of Jan de Hartog

by Arthur Myers

Most authors are people of imagination. They spin their characters, settings, and plots out of their minds. This is particularly true of writers of adventure stories. Few authors travel far beyond their home library. Changing a typewriter ribbon will give most writers enough exercise for a week. The adventurer and the writer of adventures are usually two quite different kinds of personalities.

But not always. Occasionally the poet and the adventurer inhabit the same body. An interesting example of this combination is the Dutch-American author Jan de Hartog.

De Hartog has written about the sea, about police work, about the Dutch underground fight against

the Nazis in World War II—and he has experienced all these adventures in his life. Oddly enough, his most successful work is a play about a long-married couple that was written before De Hartog married. The name of the play is "The Fourposter," and it has been translated into twenty languages. He calls the play "an adolescent's farewell to youth," a declaration of love to the woman he was yet to meet.

The greater part of De Hartog's work, however, springs from his personal adventures. His courage and deep moral principles give meaning and direction to these adventures.

Because he is the son of a minister, it is not surprising that morality has always guided De Hartog's life and work. But the adventurous side of his personality developed on its own—and at a very young age.

When De Hartog was ten years old, he ran away and became a "sea mouse." Sea mouse is a Dutch term for a certain species of small child so full of dreams, independence, and sheer overflowing energy that he or she can't help running away to sea. By Dutch law, children under 14 are not supposed to work, so the runaways would stay out of sight when the vessels were in port. Thus they were called sea mice.

Jan de Hartog did not run away because he had a bad home life. Jan's mother had been sick, and he was sent to stay at the home of a fisherman's widow. No place in Holland is far from the ocean, but Jan was suddenly so close to the sea that he simply could not resist going to work on a fishing boat.

After a few months, Jan's father found him,

brought him home, and put him back in school. But at 12, Jan ran off again, hiding on a ship bound for the Baltic Sea. His father caught up with Jan before the ship sailed. This time, Jan's father confined himself to urging the ship's officers to work Jan so hard that the boy would never want to go on another sea voyage. However, Jan quickly became a favorite with the crew. They made life so pleasant for him that Jan quickly decided to make the sea his life.

When he was 16, Jan applied to and was accepted by the Amsterdam Naval College. He was an extremely independent and lively young fellow—a bit too lively in fact. Jan was not shy about criticizing the powers-that-be, and the authorities at the naval school tossed him out within three months. When he left, Jan was told, "This school is not for pirates!"

Jan then joined the crews of oceangoing tugboats, a fleet known as "Holland's Glory." Soon thereafter, he passed the examination for mate. He was also interested in writing and hoped that life at sea would give him enough spare time to produce stories.

Although sea life was attractive in many ways, it was most demanding of his time. Jan did not get a chance to write until the early 1930s, when hard times struck and the company he worked for was forced to sell its ships. Jan found a job with the Amsterdam Harbor Police, keeping night watch in the wheelhouse of a police patrol boat.

It was a low-paying job, but it turned out to be a fine opportunity for a would-be author. Jan already knew a great deal about life at sea and was quickly learning something of police work. Before long, he was writing exciting stories of the sea and the harbor patrol. They caught the eye of the publisher of an Amsterdam newspaper, and Jan became a regularly published author.

The stories proved to be an introduction into yet another inviting field. The head of the Amsterdam Municipal Theater was working on a play about sailing ships when he happened to read one of Jan's stories.

"Here's an old salt who can give us technical advice," the man thought. He was a bit startled when the "old salt" proved to be not quite 20 years old. Jan was given a part in the play and stayed on to become a jack-of-all-trades around the theater. Before long, Jan was writing plays, as well as detective stories, and a book about another setting of which he had some experience—a naval college. Soon he went back to sea as a tugboat mate, writing when he had the chance. He managed to live in the two worlds he found so attractive, literature and the sea.

Then World War II broke out, and Holland was one of the first countries the Germans invaded. At the time, De Hartog was working on his first really important book, called *Holland's Glory.* It was a tale of the seagoing tugs.

Although the Dutch military defense was doomed from the start, the nation was finding other ways of resisting the German conquest. The Dutch took great pride in their tugboats, which were used to help people escape to England, among other things. De Hartog was a known member of the Resistance and his book about the tugboats became a symbol of the Dutch effort against the Nazis. It became a best seller, which made the Nazis furious. They put the young author on their "Most Wanted" list, and De Hartog was forced to go into hiding.

He entered an old ladies' home, disguised as an aging woman with the name of "Mrs. Flyingheart." For three months he never left his room. He wrote his famous play, "The Fourposter," to pass the time and saw no one but the maid.

One day he sneaked out of the home and managed to reach Spain. After much difficulty, and with the help of Basque shepherds and the Spanish underground, he escaped to England. Because he was one of the first members of the Dutch Resistance, Jan—though absent from his country—was given an award by the Dutch government. In response to this act of defiance by the Dutch, the Nazis sentenced Jan de Hartog to death. Meanwhile, in England, Jan joined the Dutch merchant fleet. He left the service at the end of the war with the rank of captain.

After the war, encouraged by the success of *Holland's Glory,* De Hartog decided to write full time. His first book in the English language was *The Lost Sea.* It is a moving adventure story about an orphan boy who becomes a sea mouse on a fishing boat. Another book that gained wide readership was *The Distant Shore.* This is a war story about the Dutch tugboat fleet that, unarmed, brought crippled British ships to their home shores.

De Hartog married and began raising a family. He bought an oceangoing fishing boat and made it over into a houseboat. With his growing family, he sailed it from port to port in Europe. During the 1953 floods in Holland, the De Hartogs turned their home into a floating hospital. From this experience, De Hartog produced a book titled *The Little Ark*.

His World War II experiences are the subject of much of De Hartog's later work. *The Inspector,* for example, tells the story of a Dutch police inspector who safely guides a war-scarred Dutch Jewish girl through many dangers to Palestine. His play, "Skipper Next to God," tells of the efforts of a Dutch sea captain to land his "cargo" of fleeing Jews in a free country.

During the 1950s, De Hartog brought his houseboat across the Atlantic and explored the eastern coast of the United States.

Later he went to Houston, where he taught writing at the University of Houston. In addition, he and his wife, who are Quakers, worked as volunteers in a county hospital. Angered by the overcrowding, and the small number of doctors and nurses, he wrote *The Hospital.* In this book he exposed the miserable conditions at the hospital. As a result, an indignant public forced the officials to improve conditions there.

De Hartog and his wife also became active in a Quaker effort to help Vietnamese and Korean orphans. They themselves adopted two Korean girls. Out of this experience came a book of advice and encouragement for people who have brought such children into their families.

And so, perhaps more than is the case with other writers of fiction books, De Hartog's books are a record of his life—a life of both adventure and genuine moral substance.

A reporter gets more than she bargained for when she spends...

A NIGHT WITH THE DUCHESS

by Sarah Lang

I almost couldn't believe my eyes when I saw a letter from the Duchess of Reardon sitting in my mailbox. One of my assignments as a reporter for my hometown newspaper is to research and write about extremely wealthy people in the area. I had sent off a note to the Duchess, asking if I might interview her. But I didn't really expect an answer.

Everyone knew the Duchess lived in the fortress-like house on top of the hill just outside town, but very few people knew anything about her. The townspeople said she was a nasty old woman who didn't care about people, only money. Still, from the time I was a child, I'd wanted to meet the person who owned that house. I was to get that chance at last.

I opened the letter and gasped. The Duchess not only agreed to the interview, but she also invited me to spend a weekend with her at the end of January. That was only two weeks away! I immediately wrote and mailed my acceptance. Then I called the publisher of my newspaper to tell him the good news.

"You're more courageous than I am, Selena," was his reply. "I've heard that the old lady is as mean as a mad dog. Not only that, people say that strange things go on in that house."

I laughed with confidence at his worries, and explained my long-standing ambition to meet the Duchess of Reardon. Still, when I got off the telephone, I wondered for a moment if my ambition was going to get me into trouble.

The next two weeks passed slowly. The weekend of my visit with the Duchess finally arrived. I was to appear at six o'clock on Friday night, in time for dinner, and leave on Sunday morning. Little did I know, as I planned all the questions I would ask the Duchess, how long even one night could be!

I drove up the long, winding road to the Reardon place. The fortresslike house stood all alone at the top of a hill, which was surrounded by a huge stone wall. Like the wall, the house was built of stone. As I arrived at Reardon, night was falling and dark clouds were forming in the sky. A stiff wind whipped me as I stepped out of my car. It was going to be a cold, stormy January night, I thought. I hoped there would be a nice fire in the fireplace to warm the Duchess and me as we talked.

I used the big, old-fashioned brass knocker on the front door to announce my arrival. Minutes went by while I waited for someone to answer the knock. Believe me, it was cold up on that hill—cold, and a bit creepy, with the wind howling through the trees. I thought then of all the terrible things I'd heard about the Duchess and wondered if this was the beginning of a weekend of torture.

Finally, the door was opened by a little old woman with a wrinkled face and stooped shoulders. She introduced herself as Margaret, a servant. As Margaret showed me the way to the living room, she explained that she had been the Duchess's companion since they were children. Margaret told me other things, too, but I hardly listened, I was so surprised by the inside of the house. We walked through three large rooms, each one more shabby than the last, before we came to the living room. Paint was peeling from all the walls, and the rooms had almost no furniture. Was this the house of a wealthy person?

We entered the living room. Seated on a small sofa was the Duchess. This time I wasn't disappointed, for she was a majestic-looking woman, even at the age of seventy. Her white hair was piled on top of her head and she was dressed in a beautiful white robe. I was most struck, though, by the sadness about her eyes and mouth. I realized that she must have suffered deeply in her life.

A storm raged outside as the Duchess and I shared a simple meal, served by Margaret. The Duchess was as courteous as I could have wished, though not exactly talkative. She was more interested in hearing about my life and the goings on in town than in talking about herself. At the time, I didn't care. I was just glad to find that she was normal, and not the horrible person I'd been led to expect. After dinner, she told me a little about the history of Reardon, then went off to bed.

I would have liked to explore the house a bit on my own, but Margaret showed me to my bedroom and wished me good night. When I asked if I could go back downstairs, Margaret cautiously said I wouldn't like it down there by myself. The warning

note in her voice did not escape me. The house was awfully cold, and so I climbed under the feather-filled covers of the bed with no further argument.

Three hours later—around midnight—I awoke, shivering with cold. The wind had blown open the windows. I was getting up to lock them when I heard urgent whispers in the hall outside my room. I heard Margaret's voice saying, "He's here, I saw him!"

The Duchess whispered back, "The storm...he came because of the storm."

Aha! Here was my chance for a good story! I waited until I heard the two of them go downstairs before I jumped out of bed. At that moment, the door to my room opened. I didn't see anything, but suddenly the room felt even colder than before. Then I heard a man's voice right next to my ear. The voice pleaded: "It's so cold outside. I'll freeze out there. Please, please let me stay." The Duchess appeared at my door and the voice faded away. I saw her for only a moment before I fainted.

When I came to, I was in the Duchess's bedroom. A fire was blazing in the fireplace, and the room was warm and cozy. The Duchess sat by the fireplace, watching me. When she was sure that I was all right, she said, "Selena, I am old and I want someone to hear my story before I die. Maybe others will learn from it.

"I once had a twin brother," the Duchess began. "He and I were very close, until at the age of sixteen he decided to leave this house. He was ashamed that we had so much wealth, while other people had so little. And he felt disdain for me because I enjoyed the privileges that money could bring. He left Reardon, saying that he was going to become a poet. He would live in poverty and write poems about the life of the poor.

"I was very hurt when my brother left," the Duchess continued, "and I vowed I would never speak to him again. After a few years, I almost forgot that I'd ever had a brother. My parents died, and I inherited this house and a great deal of money.

"Some months later, I gave a big party here at Reardon. It was a stormy night in January, just like tonight. Inside, though, it was warm and cheerful. Oh, I was happy! About midnight, a beggar came to the door and asked if he could stay the night. He had nowhere else to go. Margaret came to ask me if he could, and I said no. I never let beggars in the door. Margaret came back a few minutes later and whispered to me that the beggar said he was my brother. Still I wouldn't yield. My pride wouldn't let me forgive my brother for hurting me. Margaret turned him out into the night.

"The next day, my brother was found frozen underneath a tree a little ways down the hill. He had died of the cold, and probably of hunger too. Since that fatal day, I've given most of my fortune to the poor. I've talked to almost no one except Margaret. To this day, on the worst winter nights, my brother's ghost comes back to haunt me. That's what—or whom—you felt in your room earlier."

The Duchess had only one more thing to say. "Go home tomorrow, Selena," she advised me. "I have told you the only important thing there is to know about me. It will make a good story. Why, there's even a moral to it. Just do me one favor— wait until after I'm gone to write it."

I promised I would and left Reardon early the next day.

I have kept the promise I made to the Duchess that night. Ten years have gone by, and yesterday the Duchess died. Tomorrow, her story will be told in our newspaper. Maybe then she and her brother will rest in peace.

The destination was glory for the young fliers in...

The Lafayette Escadrille

by Arthur Myers

Throughout history, war has been one of men's favorite games. And perhaps there has never been a more exciting war toy than the airplane.

Orville and Wilbur Wright sent the first heavier-than-air flying machine fluttering into the air in 1903. Eleven years later, World War I began. By that time aviation had advanced to a point where Germany, France, and England could, among them, put 2,000 fighting planes into the air. This is a remarkable example of the progress that can occur when destruction is the goal.

At first the generals used the new aircraft for scouting purposes. The young aviators, helmeted and goggled, peered down warily from their open cockpits, zigzagging to avoid ground fire. Their job was to bring back reports on the movement of troops. On occasion, they would dump out literature that urged the enemy to forget the whole thing and go home.

Apparently, the generals hadn't considered the possibility that airplanes could be used as weapons. But the young pilots certainly did. Soon pistols and rifles were regular equipment in every cockpit, and the young aviators from opposing sides began exchanging pot shots. Before long, a Dutchman named Fokker figured out how to make a machine gun fire through the blades of a whirling propeller, and then the fun really began.

Soon the aviators were shooting each other down with the greatest of youthful energy. The gallant duel in the sky became the fancy of youth in the entire civilized world, the privilege of few but the dream of millions. Fighter pilots such as Baron Manfred von Richthofen of Germany, who bagged 80 victims before meeting his own fiery end, became a great hero—at least to the people on his own side. He led a squadron called The Flying Circus. He himself was termed The Red Baron—yes, the very Red Baron of Snoopy's dreams!

Before long there was also an American air hero, Captain Eddie Rickenbacker. Rickenbacker, however, limped along behind the leaders with a relatively poor record of shooting down 21 aircraft and 4 balloons. Of course, Rickenbacker had an excuse for his poor showing: the United States didn't get into the war until 1917. On the other hand, Rickenbacker—as well as a number of other American pilots—was fighting well before then.

Most of the American pilots who entered the war early were members of the Lafayette Escadrille. This was an American branch of the French air corps. They were young men of daring, who held great disdain for danger. They were not the sort to ponder the benefits of living to a comfortable old age. Perhaps an excellent example of life in the Escadrille is the first—and almost last—taste of combat of James Norman Hall.

Hall was an American who'd come back from fighting in the trenches with the British army. He wrote a book about his experiences that made him a well-known young author. A publisher wanted him to write about the Lafayette Escadrille.

Hall approached the leaders of the Escadrille, who were delighted with his interest. They invited Hall to join the Escadrille and thus experience the story first hand. At the age of 28, Hall was afraid he was too old—wartime pilots tended to be little older than schoolboys. Nevertheless, in the fall of 1916, Hall became a student pilot in France, and by the middle of 1917 his teachers judged him ready for action. Hall joined the Escadrille; his destination —glory.

Jimmy Hall quickly became popular with his fellow pilots. One of them wrote in later years: "Jim Hall was one of the finest all-around persons I have ever known. He had just about everything—intelligence, courage, looks, talents of many kinds, and he was a most modest man."

Hall was given a war-weary, beat-up Spad, a British airplane used by the Escadrille. He flew a couple of defense missions in this hand-me-down wreck. Then his name went up for a late-afternoon flight. In front of the hangars, the six pilots who were to fly the formation into battle received their instructions. They were to take off and attack a nearby enemy headquarters building. Hall was told to stick close to the others since this was only his third time across enemy lines.

The other planes got off all right, but Hall's ancient machine would not start. Ten minutes later, the engine finally caught. Hall lumbered into the air, bound for whatever Lady Luck might have in store for him.

Jim Hall ran into a problem immediately: he couldn't find the rest of the formation. He decided to fly around and see what was going on. He saw a couple of British planes diving at big guns on the ground. Another plane was making passes and shooting at a kite balloon. A number of pilots were flying around observing the situation below, getting information for their various headquarters. However, Hall's own squadron of Spads seemed nowhere in sight. But at least there did not seem to be enemy planes around either.

Suddenly Hall spotted a number of black specks in a neat formation about six miles (10 kilometers) inside the German lines. After studying them for a few seconds, he was sure they were his squadron. He nosed around the other airplanes and headed for the distant specks. Then he noticed that there were six—not five—planes in the squadron. But on quick reflection, he decided that some other pilot had joined up. The more the merrier, he figured.

Hall timed his turn-in beautifully, and came around to nose in for a space in the formation. Then he realized that these planes had very narrow lower wings. Only after edging one of the pilots over, did he notice that none of the planes carried the Escadrille's

Indian-head markings. In fact, they were decorated with black-barred crosses.

The truth suddenly dawned on Hall: he had joined a squadron of German Albatross planes! Pilots in black helmets and huge goggles stared at him unbelievingly. For an instant, Hall had an urge to salute, bow, and move on politely. Somehow he sensed that this was not quite the answer to his sticky problem. Hall jammed the steering stick of his airplane forward and went down like a dart. The Germans followed after him, firing all guns!

Lead tore through the wings and body of Hall's airplane. One bullet grazed his forehead, another cut across his chest, a third pierced his shoulder. Hall passed out. His speed was so great that the Germans stopped following, certain that he would never pull out of his dive. But Hall came to for a few seconds, shut off the engine, and pulled back on the stick. The airplane came out of its dive and Hall passed out again.

Lady Luck then seemed to take over as Hall's co-pilot. The wings stayed on, and the plane went into a turning glide. One minute the airplane was heading for the German lines, the next minute it was heading for home. Lady Luck piloted the plane back over to the French lines, and even landed the ship for Hall, for he was still unconscious.

When Hall finally came to, he was lying on a stretcher and was being carried away from the trench area. He squinted at the stretcher bearers, unsure whether they were German or French. Then he saw that one of the soldiers was wearing a French steel helmet, not a German "coal bucket." Through no fault of his own, Hall had made it home.

And so, Jim Hall lived to fight another day—in fact, almost another year. In May of 1918, while on a flight with two other pilots, one of them the famed Rickenbacker, Hall's plane began to come apart during an air battle. He tried to get back over the front lines, but was hit by German ground fire and spun down into a field. He survived the crash, but was captured immediately.

Hall expected vicious treatment from the Germans, but found to his surprise that they were quite pleasant to him. The first words he heard from a German soldier were spoken in English as he sat in his wrecked plane, shaken up from hitting his head against the windshield.

"Are you hurt, sir?" the soldier asked courteously.

Not badly. And in the gallant custom of captured officers—Hall was a captain by then—Hall chewed up and swallowed his squadron orders. Jim Hall, the complete gentleman at arms, spent the rest of the war in a prisoners' camp.

After the war, he wrote a book about his flying experiences called *High Adventure*. Then, with another American war pilot, Charles Nordhoff, he carved an unusual writing career. Together, they moved to the South Seas and wrote some of the great entertainments of this century—the adventure books *Mutiny on the Bounty*, *Pitcairn Island*, and others.

Life was certainly a high adventure to Jimmy Hall. And in his day, war could be too—for some of the lucky ones.

The Blackbird's Flight

Part 1
by Kay Jordan

The rest of Lisa's family can accept their poverty, but she dreams of a better life.

Lisa Edwards wiped the minister's desk clean, feeling no sense of accomplishment. As she locked up the rooms, she thought of how much she hated cleaning the church offices as her weekly "gift." She would have preferred to put money in the church's collection plate like everyone else. However, the Edwards family had little money, and certainly none to spare. Lisa's mother believed that being allowed to give of their time was a privilege.

Lisa hated being poor. Although she knew everyone respected her family for working so hard, Lisa couldn't help feeling disdain for her poverty.

Before she walked out of the building, Lisa glanced at the bulletin board posted inside the door. She saw the quotation: "I will lift up mine eyes unto the hills." She stepped outdoors. "Some hills," she thought as she viewed stacks of garbage cans piled high with papers and wine bottles. Then she hurried on her way.

Lisa's neighborhood had once been a wealthy area of Dallas and still bordered an established section with good schools and well-known churches. Unable to afford better housing, Mrs. Edwards had chosen the bordering location so that her children could attend the better schools. Lisa, however, hated the neighborhood down to its last decaying brick. She longed to live in the cheap, new apartments outside the city. There, at least, everyone would be alike. She hated being poorer than her friends, and she didn't accept her mother's idea that honesty and ambition were more important than money.

Lisa's feelings caused many arguments with her older sister, Marie, who never minded being the "poor church mouse." Lisa had almost died of shame when Marie gladly accepted clothing given by the church women. Lisa received no support from her brother, Jerry, either. He complained about being poor but had a strong allegiance to their mother. Besides, he seemed to like being taken under everyone's wing. Lisa was an alien in her own family.

She climbed the steps of the Summit Apartments quietly, so that Mrs. Conners, the manager, couldn't hear. But no sooner had her foot stepped on the broken tile floor of the hallway than Mrs. Conners came out.

"Lisa, a man was here looking for your mother," Mrs. Conners said. "I asked what he wanted. He said he was a relative in town for the day, and wanted to know when someone would be home. I played dumb and said I didn't know. He put a note in your mailbox. Have you any idea who he was?"

"No, we weren't expecting company," Lisa answered.

"Well, let me know if he was a fake. I'll call the police the next time."

Lisa took the note out of the mailbox and hurried up to their third-floor apartment, threw open the door, and rushed to the room she shared with her mother. She wanted to have time for her personal ceremony before anyone came home. No one knew about it, and Lisa thought her family would only laugh at her if they saw her.

Lisa put on a record and listened to "Blackbird singing in the dead of night." When it came to the part about "fly away," she pulled out the photograph from under her bed and set it against her pillow. She sat very still, listening to the song and thinking about the faded photograph of the father she was said to resemble.

Lisa didn't remember her father. He had walked out on them when she was two years old. She always thought how different life would have been if he had never left. She knew that he never sent money, called, or even wrote. But she needed the man in the picture, and she had a hard time accepting the fact that he had deserted them. Her mother never discussed him, which made Lisa suspicious that her mother had something to do with his

leaving. When the record ended, Lisa wiped away a tear and hid the picture.

Lisa then went to the phone and called her friend Kathy to report that she had asked Mike McClure to the girl-ask-boy dance. Lisa didn't want to go to the dance. She didn't have a dress or money for the meals before and after the dance, but her friends had pressured her to go.

The local gossip was that Mike wanted to date Lisa, and the girls thought this was her chance to encourage him. Even Lisa's mother wanted her to go, and Lisa had made the mistake of talking with Kathy about the dance in front of her mother. When Kathy had offered to lend Lisa a dress, her mother had accepted for Lisa. Lisa became furious. Her mother always had to interfere. After Kathy left, Lisa started an argument about money, but her mother calmly responded that she would give Lisa twenty dollars for the dance from her next paycheck.

Lisa calmly told Kathy the news. Kathy went on and on about the restaurants the girls were considering for the dinner before the dance and the breakfast the next morning. As she listened to Kathy recite the names, Lisa became more and more uncomfortable. Although she had learned to be cunning where money was concerned, Lisa knew she wasn't skillful enough to get two meals for twenty dollars at those places. Before she could betray her fear, Lisa said good-by.

Lisa told her mother about the date as soon as her mother came home. Mrs. Edwards looked pleased. She liked Lisa's friends, and she wanted Lisa to have a nice boyfriend. Lisa had forgotten about the note from the stranger until her mother asked about mail. Lisa handed her the note. Her mother read it, then quickly dialed the telephone. Lisa heard her talking to someone whose name she didn't know.

Mrs. Edwards said afterwards, "That was Fred, your father's brother. He's in town on a truck run.

Aunt Louise gave him our address. He said that your father has married again and has several children. He runs a boat for hire at a place called Nature's Corners in Florida."

The mention of her father brought Lisa's heart to her throat. She was discouraged, though, about the news of other children.

"Did he say anything else?" Lisa asked.

"No."

The sound of steps on the landing interrupted their conversation. Jerry came in with Mr. Hansen, the local grocer. Jerry was upset.

"Mrs. Edwards," the grocer said, "Jerry broke one of my front windows. It was not a mischievous prank, just a mistake. It will cost 40 dollars to replace. He can work some to pay for a part of it, but I need to have some money. I sure am sorry to come here, but I had no choice."

Dignified as usual, Mrs. Edwards took twenty dollars from her purse. "I'm sorry," she said. "We'll pay the rest when we can. Jerry will stop by tomorrow to see about work."

Lisa had a sinking feeling the moment she saw her mother give the money to the grocer. After Mr. Hansen left, Lisa yelled at Jerry, "How could you?"

"Butt out, Lisa!"

"No, I won't! That twenty dollars was to go for my date to the spring dance. Wasn't it, Mother?"

"I'm afraid it was," Mrs. Edwards answered.

"Now what will I do?" Lisa moaned. "Sell matches on the street?"

"Don't be rude," her mother said. "Jerry didn't mean it, and you still have a dress and a date."

"Correction! Kathy has a dress, which you made me take. I never wanted to go in the first place."

"Lisa, please be mature," her mother pleaded. "If Mike really wants to go to the dance with you, he won't mind missing dinner. Just tell him the truth and that we are all very sorry. I can fix breakfast for all of you back here."

"Mother! No one wants to eat at someone's home, much less this place," Lisa said acidly. "I've told you a billion times that I don't like bringing my friends to this dump."

"This dump is your home, the only home we can afford."

"That is a lie," Lisa snapped back. "We could afford the new apartments outside the city. But don't worry, I know how to lie too. I'll take care of this!"

Lisa went to the telephone and called Mike. She told him that her family had to go out of town the night of the dance to visit a sick relative.

Lisa hung up and her mother said, "You don't make yourself attractive by being a liar. People can always unravel lies and see through to the truth. Just be yourself and anyone will accept you."

"Mother, the truth is that I'm tired of being the object of everyone's pity. I'm not Cinderella, and you are not the fairy godmother."

Lisa stormed out of the room. She went into the bedroom, pulled out a book of maps, and looked up Nature's Corners, Florida. Then she got out a pen and paper.

End of Part 1

Lisa gets more than she bargained for when she visits her father. More, and less.

The Blackbird's Flight

Part 2
by Kay Jordan

The letter with the bus fare to Florida arrived three weeks before school ended. No one knew Lisa had written her father, and she didn't know how to tell her mother the sheer pleasure her father's invitation had given her. Finally, Lisa simply handed her mother the letter.

"It's against my better judgment to let you leave," Mrs. Edwards said, "but I won't stand in your way."

Lisa's older sister, Marie, and her brother, Jerry, thought Lisa was stupid to go for the whole summer. Marie couldn't resist saying, "I bet Dad just wants a cheap baby-sitter." But Lisa believed she was doing the sensible thing. When she boarded the bus three weeks later, she knew she was heading for the most important appointment of her life.

118

Lisa's dreams and plans evaporated the day she arrived in Florida, leaving her to face the biggest error of her young life. She had expected to be met by the man in the photograph, grown older, naturally, but still the handsome blond-haired man. Instead, no one was waiting at the bus station. Lisa waited for hours before her father finally arrived. Dirty and unshaven, he marched into the station and called out, "You Lisa?"

They traveled from the station to Nature's Corners in his new, but messy, station wagon. Lisa tried to talk to her father over the yelling of her three stepbrothers, who crawled all over her and the car. But he paid so little attention that she soon became quiet.

Lisa did enjoy what she could see of the swampland they passed, but her excitement dissolved into disappointment when she saw Nature's Corners. The town looked harsh and backward. Its largest building had "Marine Sales" written across the front. Weather-beaten fishing boats were moored in the water.

Before driving home, Lisa's father stopped by the bait house and made arrangments for Lisa to start work there the following morning. Although she had hoped that they would first spend some time together, she did not complain. Lisa did indicate that she knew nothing about bait or fishing, but her father simply said, "You'll learn." Then he told Lisa that she would be expected to work only in the mornings, and Lisa thought that meant she would go out with him on his boat in the afternoons. She quickly realized she was wrong again when he added, "Hazel wants you to help out at home in the afternoons."

Lisa learned quickly that she hated everything connected with fishing. The rank smell of the bait shack almost made her sick, and Jack, the owner, was always complaining. She tried to get him to teach her about boats, but he only got as far as pointing out the difference between aft and prow.

Lisa didn't like the fishermen who came into the place either. They were all older than she, and Lisa was convinced that there wasn't a teen-ager in the vicinity. Most of the men were polite, but one or two made passes at her. When she complained to her father, he said that she had to learn to stand on her own feet. His total lack of concern hurt. She fought hard to conceal her tears.

Spending time at her father's home was even worse than the bait shop. Lisa didn't really like Hazel, and they had nothing to say to each other. Hazel often went to visit a neighbor, leaving Lisa to care for the three young children. Their favorite sport was to rush and tackle Lisa.

Lisa spent her first weeks in Nature's Corners trying hard to maintain control of herself. She didn't notice until later that her father's life was not in rhythm with the rest of the fishing community. He often as not stayed home, giving feeble excuses for not going fishing.

Then one afternoon a yacht docked at the wharf. Its owner came ashore that evening to visit Lisa's father. Lisa noticed that although the man didn't dress like the locals, he acted as if he belonged in the area. Something about the man frightened Lisa. She watched her father and the yacht owner walk out into the yard, where they spent an hour talking in low tones.

Late that night, Lisa heard her father pull out of the driveway. Then, around midnight, she heard a small plane fly in low over the house. The next morning she asked her father about the aircraft. He uttered an oath and harshly told her, "You didn't hear nothing."

His remark hurt and Lisa didn't bother asking questions again, but she began to watch his actions. She noticed that her father would carefully read only one section of the newspaper. He also listened to the nightly news—for the fishing reports, he said. But she saw his face tighten the day a reporter said that a boat carrying a big drug shipment had been captured beyond the reef.

Lisa heard several more low-flying aircraft on following nights. Her father was always absent those nights, but he would always be standing by the car the next morning to make sure she went off to work. Suddenly everything was all too clear. Her father's hours, the suspicious aircraft, the always available money, added up to only one thing: drugs. Lisa was sure the planes delivered drugs, which her father picked up and stashed in his car. Then he had her drive the car to work and park it out of sight behind the bait house. No doubt, someone picked up the shipment of drugs while Lisa was busy working inside.

Lisa began to plan. She started saving little bits of her paycheck. She took her suitcase to the bait shop and hid it, bringing an extra piece of clothing to the place a day at a time. She had almost completed her preparations for escaping when she overheard her father and the yacht owner talking behind the bait house.

"Do you think she'll go?" the owner asked. "She'll make a great cover. With her on deck, no one would suspect us of smuggling."

"Don't worry," her father answered. "Lisa's been begging to go on a boat. Besides, she'll do anything I ask."

Lisa didn't listen to the rest. She knew she had to act fast. She was smart enough to know that her father didn't really care what happened to her.

Lisa left work that day at the normal hour. She drove home, grabbed her money, and told Hazel that she had to run an errand for Jack, the bait-shop owner. Then she drove straight to the bus station. She put the car keys in an envelope and mailed them to her father. She did not enclose a note with the keys. She walked away from her father without a single good-by, just as he had walked away from her years before.

As the bus headed to its destination, Lisa tried to submerge her feelings of hurt, betrayal, and shame. Over and over, she told herself that she got only what she deserved. Somehow that knowledge did not ease the pain.

Tears formed in her eyes as Lisa climbed the worn steps of the Summit Apartments. Mrs. Edwards answered Lisa's knock and Lisa fell into her mother's arms, sobbing. Lisa had hoped she would feel better about being home after her horrible experience in Florida. After one look around the apartment, she knew that she would always hate it, regardless of how much she tried to accept it.

That night Lisa and her mother talked about the man who had tormented them both. Lisa's mother admitted that her ex-husband had never taken any responsibility for the family. When he left he took with him their total bank deposit. Nevertheless, Lisa's mother never criticized the man in front of her children. "To have told you about his shabby behavior would have done none of us any good," Mrs. Edwards said. "I know that our life is hard for you to accept, Lisa. I've fumbled badly with you. That's why I wanted you to have that man in the photograph, not the real man."

"So you know about my personal ceremony of playing the 'Blackbird' record and looking at Dad's photograph?"

"Yes, I walked in one day and saw you," Mrs. Edwards admitted. "But I know you need dreams. You're not like Jerry and Marie, who accept the reality of their lives without pain. Being poor will always embarrass you, won't it?"

"I'm afraid so, Mom."

"Well, one day, you will fly away—just like the blackbird in your record. And maybe, when you are older, you might even understand what I've been trying to teach you. Besides, as you once said, I'm no fairy godmother."

"Yes, but you sure beat the wicked stepmother," Lisa answered. Then she stood up and went to play "Blackbird." But this time, Lisa left her father's photograph buried under the bed.

Giacomo Puccini

by Arthur Myers

He rose from poverty to become one of the great names in music.

He was tall, handsome, and dignified. He looked more like the hero of an opera than the composer of operas that he was. In the early twentieth century, he was probably the most famous living musician in the world. His name was Giacomo Puccini.

Puccini lived in a small village in Italy. In spite of his musical genius and his fabled accomplishments, he liked to think of himself as a simple man. He encouraged the world to regard him that way too.

"I hate palaces!" he once wrote. "I hate capitals! I hate styles! I hate top hats and evening clothes!"

Puccini preferred to think of himself as a sports-man rather than as a famous musician. Duck hunting was a favorite sport of his. He often sat through the chill of wet mornings in a duck blind on a lake near his house. Afterward he would go home and write pages of triumphant notes that made him known wherever music was heard. His operas— among them *Madame Butterfly, La Bohème, Tosca, Manon Lescaut*—are famous throughout the world.

Around the turn of the century, however, the United States was still a shade behind the times—in artistic knowledge, that is. In 1906, Puccini's two most famous works, *Madame Butterfly* and *Manon Lescaut*, had never been heard at the nation's great fortress of the musical arts: the Metropolitan Opera House in New York City. The time had come, leaders of musical taste decided, to repair that failure. Not only would the Metropolitan put on these operas, but Puccini himself would be invited to come to New York to see the singers rehearse, and to be present at the first public performances.

And so, on January 18, 1907, the 49-year-old

Puccini came down the gangplank of a ship docked in New York as thousands cheered. An army of newspaper reporters fought to get within hailing distance of the great musician.

By this time, Puccini was in rather a tense mood. His ship had been fogbound in New York Harbor for 24 hours, and he had already missed the preparations for *Manon Lescaut*. The first performance was to go on that evening, and Puccini was in a great hurry to get to the Metropolitan. He was not in too much of a hurry, however, to give the reporters a magnificent scoop—the man was a genius at public relations as well as music. He was planning, Puccini announced, to write an opera about the American West.

Having delivered himself of this news, Puccini—accompanied by his wife and grown son—hurried to his hotel, and then on to the Metropolitan.

By the time Puccini arrived at the opera house, the show had already started. He quietly slipped into his box. When the lights came up at the end of the first act, the public saw their idol for the first time. The audience broke into a storm of applause that lasted a full 10 minutes. Puccini responded courteously throughout the demonstration, bowing again and again. "Everytime there was applause," he said later, "I had to get up and sit down. I felt like one of those puppets you see at the circus."

The next morning, Puccini began to explore New York City. He loved the fast pace and excitement of the American scene. He was fascinated by American automobiles and other machinery—and also by American women. He was a gallant of the old school, and certainly not a man to disdain a pretty face and figure.

He attended rehearsals at the Metropolitan and there met old friends—the great singer Enrico Caruso and Caruso's close friend, the singer Antonio Scotti. Soon the three men were seldom seen apart.

They had in common not only a great love for music, but also a background of severe poverty. Puccini's mother had been forced to beg in the streets of the Italian city of Lucca in order to give her son his musical education. Caruso was the son of a common laborer.

There were others at the Metropolitan who had known poverty. Arturo Toscanini, the great orchestra conductor at the Metropolitan, was the son of a poor tailor. One of the great women singers of the time, Lina Cavalieri, owned jewels worth $3,000,000, given to her by noble admirers. But the singer never forgot that as a child she had slept in doorways and begged for scraps of bread to share with her mother, a washerwoman.

Music had brought them fame and riches, but these people never could shake the fear that the wheel of fortune might suddenly betray them and leave them penniless again. They stuck together as though for comfort, each understanding the other's unspoken fear.

Although he devoted the major part of his time to work, family, and friends, Puccini still found time to chase after pretty young American women connected with the Metropolitan. This involved a certain amount of dodging around backstage corners

and wardrobe rooms.

Eventually Puccini's friend, Caruso, told Elvira
Puccini about her husband's hobby. It was the
singer's way of getting even for dozens of practical
jokes Puccini had played on him over the years. Mrs.
Puccini lowered the boom and, in a public scene,
forced one lady to give back a ring that Puccini had
given her. From then on, Puccini's wife kept a sharp
eye peeled on him, to such a degree that Puccini

began to suspect she had unusual powers. He became convinced that his wife was psychic after she found a note from a lady that he had hidden in the band of his hat.

"Don't tell me Elvira is not a medium," he said over and over, "for how else could she have seen through that hatband?"

Puccini found a way to get even with Caruso. Every night Puccini, Caruso, and Scotti would play cards in a restaurant in the heart of Little Italy in New York City. If Caruso had not been a great singer, he would have made a great cardsharp. He often hit winning streaks that left the other players breathless. Puccini and Scotti paid the owner of the place to put a small mirror behind the chair Caruso always chose. From then on Caruso began to lose, never realizing that Puccini could see his cards and was cheating him royally. Not until Puccini was safely back in Europe did he take pity on his friend and warn Caruso of the trap. [1]

Throughout the fun and games, Puccini remained aware that he had made a vow when he had set foot on American shores. He fully intended to fulfill his promise to write an opera about America. He went to show after show in New York in his search for a play that could be set to music. Unfortunately, he rarely found even a single scene that would work as opera.

Finally, near the end of this stay, Puccini found what he was looking for. It was an old but popular show by the well-known theater man, David Belasco. It was called *Girl of the Golden West*. In a later day, the play might well have been described as a ridiculous can of corn, but it was certainly no cornier than the average opera plot. Puccini returned to Italy and went to work.

The opera—called *La Fanciulla del West*—was given its first performance at the Metropolitan in 1910, and it may well have been the greatest American public event of the year. Puccini returned to New York to see the performance and was given an even warmer greeting than before. Caruso sang the lead, and Toscanini conducted. Puccini took 55 curtain calls. He owned the town, if not the country. Still, he was not totally fulfilled.

There was one thing Puccini greatly wanted from America, and that was a wonderful motorboat he had seen in a display window on Fifth Avenue. It cost $3,000, and in those days that was too much even for a rich musician. At first he thought that he would go back to Italy disappointed. Then a friendly banker bought the boat for him—in exchange for a personally copied, autographed score (as a written piece of music is called) of "Musetta's Waltz" from *La Bohème*.

Giacomo Puccini died in 1924 before completing his last opera, *Turandot*. Using the composer's well-developed sketches, one of his students completed the score. Puccini's close friend, Arturo Toscanini, conducted its world premiere performance. When Toscanini came to the last note Puccini himself had written, he put down his baton. The astonished performers on stage stopped singing. The orchestra stopped playing. Toscanini turned, faced the confused audience, and said, "This is where the Master stopped." Then he walked out of the opera house.

black woman pilot flies the friendly skies

How would you react to getting on an airplane and finding Shirley Tyus in the pilot's seat?

Shirley Tyus is one of a small but growing number of black females working in the cockpits of the nation's commercial airlines. The first black female pilot hired at United Airlines, Tyus beams with confidence and pride as she approaches the airliner she will be flying.

Seeing a black woman walking toward an airplane dressed in a pilot's uniform turns a lot of heads, but

Tyus takes the attention in stride. When Tyus opens the door to the cockpit of a United Airlines passenger jet, some passengers watch in amazement.

Some are so determined to find out what the black woman is up to that they follow her to the door of the cockpit, where they see Tyus and three other pilots behind the controls preparing the airplane for flight. Usually, these three other pilots are white males, who make up the largest number of commercial pilots. In this field, women are rare, and women of color are even rarer.

Without hesitating—or thinking—many ask Shirley Tyus when they see her walking by in her uniform, "Are you a pilot?"

A striking woman in her navy blue uniform, Tyus stops and turns to face them. She courteously tells them that yes, she is a pilot, adding that she is a second officer and the first black female pilot hired by United Airlines. Frequently, passengers request that Tyus stand next to them while someone takes their photograph. They want to remember their meeting with this pioneer. Other passengers ask Tyus how her career began.

But while most passengers respond positively, some do not. When she saw the black female pilot preparing a Boeing 727 for flight, one woman stared at Tyus in shock. "Oh my God," the woman screamed in front of the entire crew. "Are *you* the pilot?"

Fortunately, most passengers are happy to meet the pioneering pilot, even if they are surprised. And Tyus, 41, who lives in Washington, D.C., with her husband and three children, understands why people have a hard time concealing their surprise.

After all, there are only four black females in United Airlines' pool of more than 7,000 pilots. That's four more black female pilots than most major U.S. commercial airline carriers employ. And 70 years after Bessie Coleman became the first black woman to earn a pilot's license, a black female commercial airline pilot is still a rare sight.

Flying an airplane requires a great deal of technical

knowledge. Being a pilot is not just a job. It is a career that requires much education, training, and preparation. To have a career as a pilot, it is essential to set a goal and work toward it over many years of preparation. Tyus says that pilots have to be very skillful, but most of all, they absolutely must have confidence in themselves. Black women pilots need to have the ambition, energy, and drive it takes to enter this demanding career.

"All of the attention over my career as a pilot is nice, but it's too bad that in 1991 there were still so few black female pilots working for major commercial airlines," says Tyus. She would like to see more black people, especially more black women, in the cockpit. She dreams of starting and running a school to train black pilots. "I look forward to the day when I won't seem strange, when people won't be surprised to see me in this uniform."

The doors to Tyus's career in aviation were first opened in 1972, when United Airlines decided to step up its program of affirmative action. Affirmative action, as the word "affirmative" suggests, means positive steps to offer opportunities to people who have been treated unfairly in the past. In the past, women and people of color were discouraged from entering many fields because of old, limited ideas and social opposition. In the 1960s and 1970s, affirmative action programs started to open these fields.

In 1972, United Airlines began its search for more black flight attendants to wait on passengers. Tyus decided to try for a position as flight attendant. She landed the job and was hired that year. Even with the excitement of the position, she soon became fascinated with the idea of what went into flying the airplane. She started asking the pilots questions about their work, and asked them to recommend good flight schools.

As Tyus shared her dream with friends, some of them expressed doubts that she could do well in a career dominated by white males. One of her friends even bet money that her dream wouldn't get off the ground. "But I never lost faith because I knew that mastering the art of flying meant believing in myself," Tyus says.

Tyus put her dream in motion in 1977, when she entered flight school in Friendly, Maryland. Her husband, Kofi, managed the home and his greeting card business while she started training for her new career.

Many of her fellow students thought that the 27-year-old flight attendant was out of place. Most of the students, as well as most of the teachers, were white males. One of Tyus's teachers didn't like the presence of a black woman. "He told me, 'If I train you, then chances are you'll get a job before I do,'" remembers Tyus, who struggled for years to earn sufficient money to pay for her training. Flight school is expensive, and Tyus ended up paying more than $30,000 for her aviation education.

Tyus completed the first stage of her dream when she earned her pilot's license in 1979. But in order to land a pilot's job with United Airlines, she needed at least 350 hours of flight time. Tyus went on to reach more than 2,000 hours of flight time as a part-time pilot for the black-owned Wheeler Airlines (now known as WRA), based in Raleigh, North Carolina.

During this time, Tyus continued working as a

flight attendant at United Airlines. She was a pilot at Wheeler Airlines during her days off and vacations. Working as a flight attendant and a pilot at the same time proved difficult. But Selena Wheeler, an official of Wheeler Airlines, which provides employment opportunities for many black pilots, says that Tyus was determined to prevail. "Shirley would fly during the day, then she would get up at two or three o'clock in the morning and fly all night," says Wheeler, adding that Tyus often slept in her home between flights. "Shirley was a very hard worker."

In 1986, Tyus tried for a position as a United Airlines pilot. Although she interviewed for the job and took part in the company's demanding screening, she was not hired. A year later, she tried for a position as pilot again, and this time she was hired, making her the first black female pilot in the history of United Airlines.

"One of the most difficult things to do when you are trying to reach your goal is to raise your head once you have already met with defeat," says Tyus. She adds that many pilots don't succeed in landing a job on their first try. "I knew that I would make it sooner or later, so I refused to let anyone or anything stand in my way," says Tyus.

Since 1987, when her career as a pilot with United Airlines began, Tyus has had many experiences she will always remember. Once she flew over the Statue of Liberty. Another time she received a thumbs-up victory gesture from Jesse Jackson, who happened to be a passenger on one of her flights. On another occasion, she shared her parents' pride in her as she took them for a joy ride in the sky.

Although Tyus works hard, she still manages to make time for her family. She enjoys reading to her daughter Ofosuwa, 4, or helping her daughter Akosua, 8, with her homework. Her oldest son, Andre, is now 22. Her children and her husband are all proud of her career as a pilot.

Besides navigating the airplane, Tyus's responsibilities include conducting inspections of the aircraft and checking the electrical and fuel systems. Concerned about safety, she also checks the instruments inside the cockpit, a task that is part of her many duties as second officer to the captain. A positive model for black women at the airlines, Tyus enjoys telling flight attendants how she started out as a flight attendant herself back in 1972. She hopes to encourage them to dream big.

Tyus still has her own dreams for the future. The determined pilot is currently taking a course that will lead to a promotion to first officer—only one seat away from the leadership of the captain's chair. And United Airlines' captains shouldn't be surprised if Tyus starts asking them questions about their careers.

Indeed, for Tyus, the sky is the limit.

Reprinted by permission of EBONY Magazine, © 1991 by Johnson Publishing Company, Inc.

Write *T* if the sentence is true; write *F* if it is false.

Fact or
Opinion

1. _____ The following sentence is an opinion: "The movie theaters of the 1920s were the greatest architectural achievements in historical memory."

Fact or
Theory

2. _____ The following sentence is a theory: "The theaters were social safety outlets because in the movie palace, the public could enjoy the luxuries usually reserved for only the rich."

Find the one correct answer.

Drawing
Conclusions

3. _____ What led historians to conclude that the Twenties were a time of opposites?
   a. There were many architectural achievements back then.
   b. There were some very, very rich people and masses of poor.
   c. There were a lot of movies being made and many temples being built.
   d. They learned from historical memory.

Recognizing
Feelings

4. _____ When the masses of the poor read about the life of the rich, how did they feel?
   a. They felt only hate.
   b. They cried for the sad fate of the rich.
   c. They longed to live like the rich, if only for a couple of hours.
   d. They were filled with joy about their fates.

5. _____ "And so was born the style that came to be known as Roxy Renaissance. It was copied by theater builders all over the United States." What does *It* in the second sentence stand for?

   a. Born
   b. Theater builders
   c. Roxy Renaissance style
   d. The United States

6. _____ Exhibitors built movie palaces because

   a. "flickers" were very popular then.
   b. kings and emperors started going to the movies.
   c. they didn't know what else to do with their money.
   d. the movie makers wanted them to provide the proper atmosphere for the movies.

7. _____ Live talent disappeared from the stage of movie theaters because

   a. talking pictures came in.
   b. a bomb killed the musicians and dancers.
   c. people lost their money in the stock market.
   d. ghosts began to haunt the movie theaters.

8. _____ The new Roxy Theater was large enough to seat

   a. a barroom full of people.
   b. the population of a small city, visiting firemen included.
   c. all the people living in Pennsylvania.
   d. the population of musicians living in New York City.

Making
Inferences

△9._____ Why does the writer call television "the death blow" to movie theaters?
  a. Only the worst movies were shown on television.
  b. People could stay home and see a movie instead of having to go to a movie theater.
  c. The people who sold television sets burned down all the movie theaters.
  d. A TV reporter proved that movie-theater owners were cheating the public.

Main Idea

(10.)_____ What is the main idea of this story?
  a. Built partly in answer to social needs, the movie palaces reflected the mood of the 1920s.
  b. Old movie houses today are haunted by ghosts.
  c. Not even buildings last forever.
  d. Poor people should not waste their money on movies.

Check your answers with the key.

FA-2 ━━━━━━━━━━━━ THE METEOR, PART 1

Find the one correct answer.

Features of a Short Story

1. _____ Who is the main character?
  a. Mr. Bradley
  b. Henry
  c. "Moose" Allen
  d. Daisy Brown

2. _____ What is the tone of this story?
  a. Very sad
  b. Very angry
  c. Funny but a little sad
  d. Scary and mysterious

3. _____ Which of the following was the most important event in the plot of the story?
   a. Moose gets benched in football.
   b. Henry thinks of digging up a meteor.
   c. Moose throws Henry into the girls' gym.
   d. Stringbean and the others disappear into shop classes.

Understanding Character

4. _____ What have you learned about Henry?
   a. He is jealous of people who are good in sports.
   b. He wants to get even with Moose and the boys.
   c. He forgives easily.
   d. He wouldn't ever think of hurting someone.

5. _____ What have you learned about Moose?
   a. He is big but kindhearted.
   b. He is a bully.
   c. He is very courageous.
   d. He protects others from harm.

Using Context Clues to Find Word Meanings

6. _____ Go back to the story to figure out which of the following gives the meaning of *revenge*:
   a. To get even with someone who has done you wrong
   b. To beat up someone smaller than you
   c. A kind of chemical
   d. A feeling of amazement

Recognizing Feelings

7. _____ At the end, how does Henry feel about Moose?
   a. Hurt and furious with Moose
   b. Warm and thankful for his friendship
   c. Jealous of Moose's abilities

d. Sad and sorry for Moose's lack of brains

Word Pictures

8. _____ What does the writer mean by saying: "After several other similar dates, Henry decided that all his dates had one thing in common: the space between their ears was filled with asphalt"?
   a. Henry's dates wore hats made of asphalt.
   b. Henry's dates liked to go for car rides on freshly paved highways.
   c. Henry's dates were not very smart.
   d. Henry's dates were all over-weight.

Predicting Outcomes

9. _____ What do you think Henry will do next?
   a. Run away from home
   b. Beat up Moose
   c. Build a rocket and send Moose into outer space
   d. Make Moose look like a fool

Main Idea

10. _____ What is the main idea of this story?
   a. Everyone is treated as an equal in a gang.
   b. Henry finally reached a point where he refused to take any more bad treatment from the gang.
   c. No matter what happens, Moose and Henry will always be the best of friends.
   d. Schools these days are having a lot of trouble with students.

Check your answers with the key.

Write *T* if the sentence is true; write *F* if it is false.

Real or
Make-Believe

1. _____ There really was a meteor buried out near the old rock quarry.

Find the one correct answer.

Making
Inferences

 _____ Why did Moose ask Henry so many questions about the meteor?
a. He loved learning about science.
b. He was afraid of doing something criminal.
c. He didn't quite trust Henry.
d. He didn't think a meteor would make a good science project.

3. _____ Why couldn't the police officers get close enough to the boys to hear their side of the story?
a. The boys smelled awful.
b. The police thought they were dangerous.
c. The expressions on the boys' faces scared the police.
d. The meteor started glowing.

Features of
a Short Story

4. _____ Which of the following was the most important event in the plot of the story?
a. Henry alone had the honor of riding to the station with the police.
b. Henry reminds the gang about the time they stole a tombstone.
c. The neighborhood meets at Henry's house.
d. Henry and Moose begin a new kind of friendship.

Sensory Images

5. _____ Which of your senses is the writer appealing to by saying: "The sound of the breaking sewer block was music to Henry's ears, as were the screams and yells from the gang"?
a. Sight   c. Touch
b. Hearing   d. Smell

Recognizing Feelings

6. _____ When the parents met at Henry's house for a neighborhood meeting, how did they feel?
a. Angry and worried
b. Happy and joyful
c. Scared and tired
d. Courageous and brave

7. _____ When his own father turned against him, how did Henry feel?
a. Ashamed   c. Furious
b. Scared   d. Happy

8. _____ How did the gang feel about Henry after the meeting?
a. They still wanted to smash his face.
b. They liked him more now that he wasn't such a wimp.
c. They were scared of Henry's getting even with them again.
d. They all thought he no longer had any brains.

Sequence of Events

9. _____ Of the following events, which one happened last?
a. The parents hold a meeting in Henry's house.
b. Moose decides to enter a calf's brain in the science fair.
c. The sewage block breaks.
d. The authorities file criminal trespass charges against the boys.

145

Main Idea   (10.)_____ What is the main idea of this
                          story?
                          a. Sewage smells awful.
                          b. Practical jokes are illegal.
                          c. People love football heros, not
                             brains.
                          d. Friends shouldn't pick on each
                             other.

Check your answers with the key.

FA-4▬▬HIGH-PROFILE WORKING MOTHERS

Find the one correct answer.

Important   1. _____ The career women in the article
Details   all agree that
                           a. their goal is to buy an expen-
                              sive car.
                           b. their schedules are not very
                              busy.
                           c. family is most important to
                              them.
                           d. their careers come first.

                2. _____ Which woman was not mentioned
                           in the article?
                           a. Anna Perez
                           b. Mary Schmidt Campbell
                           c. Barbara Green
                           d. Sundra Escott-Russell

                3. _____ Who is the pilot of the Boeing
                           727 jets?
                           a. Vanessa Bell Calloway
                           b. Dorothy Tucker
                           c. Shirley Tyus
                           d. Barbara Green

                4. _____ Which word best describes the
                           husbands mentioned in the arti-
                           cle?
                           a. Demanding   c. Lazy
                           b. Guilty   d. Supportive

146

5. _____ All the women in the article have successful jobs. Name three of these jobs.
   a. Actor, teacher, tennis player
   b. TV reporter, pilot, press secretary
   c. Artist, doctor, dishwasher
   d. Mayor, sports reporter, lawyer

6. _____ What two hit movies are mentioned in the article?
   a. *Coming to America* and *Father of the Bride*
   b. *Boyz N the Hood* and *Bugsy*
   c. *Coming to America* and *Boys N the Hood*
   d. *Father of the Bride* and *The Doctor*

7. _____ How do these mothers make more family time?
   a. They call in sick at least once a month.
   b. They take long vacations from their jobs.
   c. They attend fewer parties and weekend speaking dates.
   d. They quit their jobs.

Recognizing Feelings

8. _____ How did Dorothy Tucker feel when she received a community service award?
   a. Proud   c. Angry
   b. Scared   d. Hurt

Summarizing

9. _____ What is the best summary of this article?
   a. Six successful women are asked about their jobs and their salaries.
   b. Six successful women ask their husbands to stay at home with the children so that they may work full-time.

147

c. Six successful women talk about how they have balanced careers and families.

d. Six successful women talk about how they were hired for their important jobs.

Main Idea (10.) _____ What is the main idea of this article?

a. Women in the spotlight make a lot of money.

b. Although their lives are very busy, women in the spotlight have great social lives.

c. Women in the spotlight have found successful ways to have both a career and a family.

d. It's not easy being a woman today.

Check your answers with the key.

FA-5 ━━━━━━━━━━━━━━━━━━━━ **THE PHANTOM**

Find the one correct answer.

Features of a Short Story

1. _____ What is the setting of this story?

a. The United States at the turn of the century

b. Inside a submarine during World War II

c. In a government office last year

d. At an Air Force base during the Civil War

2. _____ Who is the main character?

a. The crew of the submarine

b. The captain

c. Sam

d. The enemy

3. _____ What is the tone of this story?

a. Happy and joyful c. Funny

b. Very angry   d. Weird

4. _____ Which of the following was the
most important event in the plot
of the story?
a. Giant flowers held *The Phantom*
near the bottom of the sea.
b. The crew had bad nerves.
c. The crew was glad for the
chance to be heroes.
d. The captain had a bad dream.

Cause
and Effect

5. _____ The enemy usually didn't pick up
The Phantom on their radar
because
a. her torpedoes came from
nowhere.
b. smoke and fire always hid her.
c. she cruised at great depths.
d. her captain and crew were
excellent.

Recognizing
Feelings

6. _____ How did the captain and crew
feel about the good luck *The
Phantom* had in the first months?
a. Great amazement
b. Very tired
c. Overcome with joy
d. Proud

7. _____ When the captain looked through
the porthole at the ocean floor
and saw the giant flowers, how
did he feel?
a. Amazed and scared
b. Angry
c. Happy and relieved
d. Cheated

Sensory
Images

8. _____ Which of your senses is the writer
appealing to by saying: "When the
vibrations from the last torpedo
hitting its target would die down,
I'd give the order to ascend"?
a. Sight   c. Touch
b. Smell   d. Taste

149

9. _____ Other submarines were spotted and attacked, whereas *The Phantom*
   a. never left port.
   b. was attacked more often than the other submarines.
   c. was never attacked.
   d. never went into enemy territory.

(10.)_____ What is the main idea of this story?
   a. Submarine crews have bad nerves.
   b. Weird flowers can be found on the ocean bottom.
   c. Mysterious flowers stopped *The Phantom* from doing any more killing.
   d. Secret missions are very dangerous.

Check your answers with the key.

FA-6 ▰▰▰▰▰ THE SUMMIT OF ANNAPURNA

Find the one correct answer.

1. _____ What did Arlene Blum do for a living?
   a. She taught mountain climbing.
   b. She was a newspaper reporter.
   c. She was a scientist.
   d. She was an artist.

2. _____ How does Annapurna I rank among the highest mountains in the world?
   a. Second
   b. First
   c. Eleventh
   d. Tenth

3. _____ They set up their base camp at 14,200 feet, but the summit of Annapurna loomed
   a. nearly two and a half vertical miles above them.
   b. only one mile above them.
   c. less than 14,200 feet above them.
   d. almost 21,000 feet above them.

Features of
a Short Story

4. _____ What is the setting of the story?
   a. The Andes Mountains in Peru
   b. The Rocky Mountains in Colorado
   c. The Himalayan Mountains of Nepal
   d. Seattle

Using Context
Clues to Find
Word Meanings

5. _____ Go back to the story to figure out which of the following gives the meaning of *tape recorder*:
   a. A measuring stick
   b. A machine that melts snow
   c. A machine that records sounds on tape and plays them back
   d. A kind of rope used in mountain climbing

Word
Pictures

6. _____ What does the writer mean by saying: "Then the mountain showed its teeth"?
   a. Annapurna bit Arlene and the other climbers.
   b. Pieces of ice that looked like teeth stuck out on Annapurna.
   c. The Dutch expedition of 1977 had carved steps that looked like teeth out of the ice.
   d. As the climbers ascended Annapurna, they discovered that the mountain was very dangerous to climb.

151

7. _____ What does the writer mean by saying: "In some places they groped along a knife blade of ice no more than 4 inches wide with gigantic drops to either side"?
   a. Mountain climbers practice by walking on knives.
   b. Mountain climbers always keep knives in their hands in case of trouble.
   c. These mountain climbers had to walk over very thin, sharp bridges of ice.
   d. Knives stick out in the snow along trails in the mountains.

Recognizing Feelings

8. _____ When Arlene went up and across Dutch Rib, how was she feeling?
   a. Very happy because they were near the summit of Annapurna
   b. Angry that an avalanche had destroyed the mess tent
   c. Very scared that she would be buried under an avalanche but still eager to get to the top
   d. Very sad for the Dutch team that had gone that way in 1977

9. _____ When Irene and Vera reached the summit, how did Arlene feel?
   a. Thrilled
   b. Cheated
   c. Terribly jealous
   d. Very sad

Main Idea

10. _____ What is the main idea of this story?
   a. Only young people should climb dangerous mountains.
   b. The climbers showed that women too can conquer one of the most dangerous mountains in the world.

c. Avalanches are exciting but dangerous to mountain climbing.
d. Mountain climbing is so easy that anyone can do it.

Check your answers with the key.

FA-7 ■■■■■■■■■■■ THE BLUE HERON FARM

Find the one correct answer.

Features of
a Short Story

1. _____ What is the setting of the story?
   a. Inside a Martian spaceship
   b. A big city
   c. A small village
   d. The Blue Heron Farm

2. _____ Who are the main characters?
   a. Sharon and Jonathan
   b. Arthur and Cindy
   c. Arthur and Charlie
   d. Steve and his wife

3. _____ What is the tone of this story?
   a. Very funny
   b. Scornful and angry
   c. Horrifying and very sad
   d. Full of warmth and love

4. _____ Which of the following was the most important event in the plot of the story?
   a. Steve's wife sees a giant lightning bolt on the way to the farm.
   b. Cindy can't start the car.
   c. Everyone runs to the root cellar to get away from the piercing noise.
   d. Hundreds of people are pulled towards the spaceship against their will.

5. _____ Why did Arthur and Cindy yell to
Steve not to turn his car off?
a. They wanted to get in the car
and escape from the farm.
b. They hated Steve and wanted
Steve and his family to get off
their land.
c. Steve had driven onto the
alfalfa field by mistake.
d. They were playing a joke on
Steve.

6. _____ Which of your senses is the writer
appealing to by saying: "We saw a
gigantic circle in the earth, as if
the field had been stamped by a
hot branding iron"?
a. Hearing   c. Smell
b. Sight   d. Taste

7. _____ "Cows, horses, pigs, goats, sheep
—even the fowl—were all moving
in one direction. They seemed to
be moving against their will, as if
drawn by some invisible force."
What does *They* in the second
sentence stand for?
a. The Martians
b. The fowl
c. All of Arthur's farm animals
d. Directions

8. _____ When the storyteller said that
she'll wait for the aliens' return,
how did she feel?
a. Happy that her family had a
chance to visit another planet
b. Scared that no one would
believe her story
c. Desperately sad at having lost
all her loved ones
d. Jealous that she had not been
chosen to go along

9. _____ What have you learned about the aliens?

a. They were peaceful and kind.
b. They were unfriendly and cruel.
c. They were totally harmless.
d. They were all terror-stricken at the sight of humans.

Main Idea

10. _____ What is the main idea of this story?

a. A woman who lost her family to aliens awaits their return.
b. Farmers never will believe in Martians.
c. The government should do more to protect everyone from aliens.
d. Aliens from outer space have already been on earth.

Check your answers with the key.

FA-8 ▬▬▬▬▬▬▬▬▬▬▬ **GHOST SHOTS**

Find the one correct answer.

Important
Details

1. _____ Gerry Gross, a meatcutter,

a. was an ordinary man in all ways.
b. took pictures of ghosts.
c. had dark hair and a full, black beard.
d. did not know how to use a camera.

2. _____ The history of photographing ghosts

a. goes back more than 100 years, to the beginning of photography.
b. was recorded by Sir Arthur Conan Doyle, a doctor and

writer.

c. begins in 1915 with Houdini's examination of Alexander Martin's photographs.

d. begins with John Myers' photographs of famous people who had died.

3. _____ "Whether or not one believes Gross's account, taking photographs of ghosts is nothing new. It goes back more than 100 years, almost to the beginning of photography." What does *It* in the second sentence stand for?

a. Ghosts

b. Gross's account

c. Taking photographs of ghosts

d. 100 years

4. _____ "Sometimes he would take photographs of families, and 'extras' would appear. These were usually the family's relatives or friends who had died." What does *These* in the second sentence stand for?

a. Families

b. Extras

c. Take and appear

d. Photographs

5. _____ "A photograph of the government council hangs in the parliament building at Victoria, British Columbia. It was taken in 1865." What does *It* in the second sentence stand for?

a. Government council

b. Building

c. Victoria, British Columbia

d. Photograph

6. _____ Go back to the story to figure out what the writer means by saying that some spirit photographers were checked by experts and received *clean bills of health*.
   a. The photographers were judged to be honest.
   b. The photographers were very healthy.
   c. The experts were all doctors of medicine.
   d. The experts charged the photographers a lot of money for their examinations.

7. _____ Go back to the story to figure out which of the following gives the meaning of *expose*:
   a. Sit still for a picture
   b. Kid the public
   c. No longer at a standstill
   d. Unmask; lay open to view

8. _____ Go back to the story to figure out which of the following gives the meaning of *activities*:
   a. Doings
   b. Ceremonies
   c. Photographs
   d. Deaths

9. _____ Go back to the story to figure out which of the following gives the meaning of *authentic*:
   a. Real
   b. Masterful
   c. Spiritlike
   d. Beautiful

157

Main Idea

(10.) _____ What is the main idea of this story?

a. Spirit photographers are cheats.
b. Spirits hover around everywhere.
c. A lot of ghosts have shown up on film over the years.
d. No one believes in ghosts anymore.

Check your answers with the key.

FA-9 ■■■■■■ THE WAY TO BECOME PRESIDENT

Find the one correct answer.

Using Context Clues to Find Word Meanings

1. _____ Go back to the story to figure out which of the following gives the meaning of *biography*:

a. A campaign speech given to voters
b. A book about the life of a real person
c. The political arts in America
d. A presidential ballot

2. _____ Go back to the story to figure out which of the following gives the meaning of *prodigy*:

a. A very ordinary youngster
b. A normal human being
c. A highly talented child
d. A child who runs for President

Important Details

3. _____ The first campaign biography in the United States was about

a. the first ten Presidents.
b. Jimmy Carter.
c. Andrew Jackson.
d. Abraham Lincoln.

Recognizing
Substitutions

4. _____ "Since that time, candidates who have managed to get their names on the presidential ballot have never failed to have a book written about them. On occasion, they have even gone to the lengths of writing that book themselves, witness Jimmy Carter's modestly titled book, *Why Not the Best?*" What does *they* in the second sentence stand for?
a. Presidential candidates
b. Biographers
c. Ballots
d. Lengths

Write *T* if the sentence is true; write *F* if it is false.

Fact or
Opinion

5. _____ The following statement is a fact: "Nothing, at least according to political wisdom, can beat a person whom voters see as being smarter than themselves—but not too much smarter."

Finding
Proof

6. _____ Look back to the story to find proof. "Thomas E. Dewey's biographer rose nobly to the occasion in his use of the just-an-average-fellow approach."

Find the one correct answer.

Making
Comparisons

7. _____ Having a widowed mother was important in politics of the 1800s, but not as important as
a. having a college education.
b. being a war hero.
c. being born in a log cabin.
d. being humble.

159

8. _____ Cal Coolidge could get more syrup out of maple trees than the other children, and Zachary Taylor
   a. was a fine fellow to have around during an Indian attack.
   b. was a college graduate.
   c. was the commanding Speaker of the House of Representatives.
   d. could, at the age of four, read adult books upside down.

Making Inferences

9. _____ Why did campaign biographers discourage any suggestion that their candidates were in the slightest degree high and mighty?
   a. Because people loved log cabins
   b. Because Rutherford B. Hayes had very bad luck
   c. Because voters liked and trusted candidates who seemed to be "just one of the people"
   d. Because no one ever voted for a candidate who went to the "University of Hard Knocks"

Main Idea

10. _____ What is the main idea of this story?
   a. Only the most ordinary people are elected to the office of President of the United States.
   b. Presidential candidates from Andrew Jackson on believed that a good campaign biography would help get them elected.
   c. Candidates today no longer do torchlight parades or give stump speeches.
   d. Candidates who hire newspaper reporters out for a fast buck never lose an election.

Check your answers with the key.

Find the one correct answer.

Understanding Character

1. _____ What have you learned about amateur football players of half a century ago?
   a. They were interested only in money.
   b. They were jealous of each other.
   c. They hated playing in the Rose Bowl.
   d. They played for fun and for applause.

2. _____ How did Riegels feel when he thought he would score a touchdown?
   a. Tired   c. Sad
   b. Silly   d. Thrilled

3. _____ How did Riegels feel when he realized that he had run in the wrong direction?
   a. Terribly embarrassed
   b. Very happy
   c. Angry at the referee
   d. Scared of Benny Lom

Features of a Short Story

4. _____ What is the setting of the story?
   a. Georgia
   b. The East Coast
   c. The Rose Bowl in Pasadena, California
   d. During World War II

5. _____ Who is the main character?
   a. Stumpy Thomason
   b. Benny Lom
   c. Roy Riegels
   d. Irv Phillips

6. _____ Which of the following was the most important event in the plot of the story?
   a. The referee blows a "quick whistle."
   b. Riegels thought a Georgia player was yelling at him to stop.
   c. Both teams scored touchdowns in the second half.
   d. Riegels picked up a loose ball and ran in the wrong direction.

7. _____ What is the tone of this story?
   a. Mysterious
   b. Sad
   c. Funny
   d. Scary

Cause and Effect

8. _____ The entire California team chased after Roy Riegels when he got the ball because
   a. the crowd was roaring too loud.
   b. Riegels was running the wrong way.
   c. Riegels was the fastest runner on the Georgia Tech team.
   d. they were happy about Riegels' touchdown.

Important Details

9. _____ When Lom tried to kick out from behind the California goal line,
   a. Roy Riegels fumbled the ball again.
   b. Georgia Tech grabbed the fumble and scored a touchdown.
   c. the ball landed behind the Georgia Tech goal and Georgia Tech was awarded two points.
   d. he kicked it clear across the field and scored two points for California.

162

Main Idea (10.)_____ What is the main idea of this story?
- a. Football is for amateurs only.
- b. The Rose Bowl isn't popular any more.
- c. Roy Riegels made one of the great "Oops, sorries" in the history of sports.
- d. Georgia Tech has always been the champion of the East.

Check your answers with the key.

FA-11 ■■■■■■■ THE SIXTH HURDLE, PART 1

Find the one correct answer.

Features of
a Short Story

1. _____ What is the setting of the story?
- a. A track field
- b. A school gym
- c. A racing meet in another state
- d. A locker room and bus stop

2. _____ Who is the main character?
- a. An Olympic runner
- b. Noah Wright
- c. Maurice Quentin
- d. Richard "Speed" Carr

Cause
and Effect

3. _____ Richard "Speed" Carr was taping his ankle because
- a. to do so helped him run faster.
- b. he had hurt it when he knocked a hurdle down.
- c. Maurice Quentin always did it.
- d. he wanted an excuse not to practice.

Important
Details

4. _____ To win a 110-meter hurdle race, you need
- a. lots of luck.
- b. speed alone.
- c. speed and perfect form.
- d. a clear head.

163

5. _____ Speed always goes over the first
five hurdles beautifully, but on the
sixth hurdle he
a. does best of all.
b. jumps too high.
c. crashes the hurdle.
d. gets tired and gives up.

6. _____ When Noah first told Speed
about Quentin running the 110-
meter hurdles in fourteen seconds,
how did Speed feel?
a. Worried about his ankle
b. Sad that Noah liked Quentin
best
c. Mad at Noah for telling him
that
d. Happy for Quentin

7. _____ Go back to the story to figure out
which of the following gives the
meaning of *doom*:
a. Losing all hope
b. Making a mistake
c. Thinking too little
d. Winning something

8. _____ What was Noah trying to do when
he shouted to Speed that Quentin
had run a 13.9?
a. Worry Speed even more
b. Get in a fight with Speed
c. Make a joke
d. Become Quentin's best friend

9. _____ What do you think Speed will do
next?
a. Have a fight with Noah
b. Hurt his ankle even more
c. Not practice anymore
d. Get over his fear of Quentin

164

Main Idea   (10.)_____ What is the main idea of this story?

a. Ants are courageous.
b. Speed's biggest problem is himself.
c. People who run hurdles have short fuses.
d. Winning, and winning alone, is all that matters to Speed.

Check your answers with the key.

FA-12 ▰▰▰▰▰▰ THE SIXTH HURDLE, PART 2

Find the one correct answer.

Sensory Images   1. _____ Which of your senses is the writer appealing to by saying: "In a grove of trees on the side of the track, a bird sprang into song"?

a. Sight
b. Hearing
c. Touch
d. Taste

Recognizing Feelings   2. _____ When Speed thought about the race, while lying on his back, how did he feel?

a. Tired from the night before
b. Sure that he would win
c. Bored with practicing all the time
d. Afraid of losing to Quentin

Using Context Clues to Find Word Meanings   3. _____ Go back to the story to figure out which of the following gives the meaning of *investigate*:

a. To raise something
b. To look closely at something
c. To tape something
d. To live

Making
Inferences

4. _____ What did Noah mean when he
told Speed not to beat himself?
   a. Speed should practice more
      often.
   b. Speed would be too tense to
      run well if he didn't stop
      worrying about Quentin.
   c. Speed should take better care
      of his ankle or he wouldn't be
      able to run the race.
   d. Speed shouldn't try to run any
      faster or he would break his
      own record.

Important
Details

5. _____ In a race, all that matters is
   a. the crowd watching.
   b. the other runners.
   c. the stopwatch.
   d. the hurdles.

Write *T* if the sentence is true; write *F* if it is false.

Real or
Make-Believe

6. _____ Speed really was running hurdles
on a track that was like molasses.

Find the one correct answer.

Cause
and Effect

7. _____ Quentin was scientific in the way
he went about hurdling because
   a. he read a lot of books about it.
   b. he used chemicals during the
      race.
   c. he carefully studied every part
      of the race.
   d. he was so explosive.

8. _____ Speed did well in his last practice
run because
   a. he had slept well the night
      before.
   b. he had taped his ankle.
   c. he thought only about the
      hurdles.
   d. his coach was timing him.

166

9. _____ What do you think Speed will do
next?
a. Lose the race
b. Knock over the sixth hurdle
c. Run the best race of his life
d. Finish in a tie with Quentin

(10.) _____ What is the main idea of this
story?
a. No one can really beat you if
you do your best.
b. Running well takes practice.
c. Winning is all that counts.
d. The sixth hurdle is the hardest
one to clear.

Check your answers with the key.

FA-13 ████████████ THE BOY WHO LIVED
WITH MONSTERS

Find the one correct answer.

1. _____ What does the writer mean by
saying: "...the distance from
Ira's nose to the TV screen was so
small, an ant with a bad back
could jump it"?
a. Ira didn't see very well.
b. Ira sat very close to the TV
screen.
c. Ira brought bugs into the
house.
d. Ira had trained an ant to jump.

2. _____ Ira kept his door shut and the
sound of the TV extremely low
because
a. monster movies scared his
mother.
b. Ira didn't want the gigantic bat
to get him.

167

c. Ira's father would yell at him if he caught Ira up at night watching TV.

d. Ira didn't want his parents to see the posters and photographs from monster movies.

Sensory Images

3. _____ Which of your senses is the writer appealing to by saying: "Ira said good-by along with Bela, carefully imitating the master's menacing tone"?
   a. Sight   c. Touch
   b. Hearing   d. Taste

Making Comparisons

4. _____ After Ira's parents fought, his mother would stay in her bedroom until late the next day, whereas his father would
   a. watch war movies in the living room.
   b. find Ira and yell at him instead.
   c. get in his car and drive away.
   d. go work in the garage.

Sequence of Events

5. _____ Of the following events, which one happened last?
   a. Ira is chased and beaten up by some tough kids in the park.
   b. Ira hides in his parents' garage.
   c. Ira gets caught in the rain.
   d. Ira is run over when his father drives the car out of the garage.

Making Inferences

6. _____ Ira's parents
   a. cared about their son a great deal.
   b. hated horror movies.
   c. didn't show Ira much love or attention.
   d. had little money to spend on movies.

168

△_____ What was Ira crying about in the garage?
  a. His lonely and painful home life
  b. The sad story in the magazine
  c. The pain in his leg
  d. The horror movie he'd miss seeing

Understanding Character

8. _____ What have you learned about Ira?
  a. He was a terrible coward and sneaked around a lot.
  b. He liked it when terrible things happened to others.
  c. He was hurt by his parents so much that only horror movies helped him forget his pain.
  d. He was jealous of other children because they had better TV sets.

Features of a Short Story

9. _____ What is the tone of the story?
  a. Happy
  b. Scary
  c. Funny
  d. Sad

Main Idea

10. _____ What is the main idea of this story?
  a. Horrible things happen only to people in the movies.
  b. Monster movies shouldn't be watched so much by young people like Ira.
  c. The monsters Ira lives with are his uncaring parents.
  d. Ira's parents were wrong to argue so much.

Check your answers with the key.

Find the one correct answer.

Cause
and Effect

1. _____ De Hartog has written about the
sea, about police work, and about
the Dutch underground fight
against the Nazis in World War II
because
   a. he knew these topics would sell
   books.
   b. he had experienced them all.
   c. he had a very good imagination.
   d. he liked reading books on these
   topics.

Using Context
Clues to Find
Word Meanings

2. _____ Go back to the story to figure out
which of the following gives the
meaning of *sea mouse*:
   a. Mice on board a ship
   b. Men who write about sailors
   c. Children who run away to sea
   d. People with overflowing energy

3. _____ Go back to the story to figure out
which of the following gives the
meaning of *response*:
   a. A punishment
   b. An escape
   c. An answer
   d. Strong anger

4. _____ Go back to the story to figure out
which of the following gives the
meaning of *defiance*:
   a. A refusal to obey
   b. Good will
   c. An award
   d. Punishment by death

Important
Details

5. _____ De Hartog's book about Holland's
seagoing tugboats

170

a. became a symbol of the Dutch resistance to the Nazis.
b. was made into a famous stage play.
c. was widely read and especially enjoyed by the Nazis.
d. was the first book in the English language.

Sequence of Events

6. _____ Of the following events, which one happened second?
a. Jan goes to work on a fishing boat.
b. Jan's father finds him and takes him back home.
c. Jan applies to and is accepted by the Amsterdam Naval College.
d. Jan runs away and sails to the Baltic Sea.

Recognizing Substitutions

7. _____ "Before long, he was writing exciting stories of the sea and the harbor patrol. They caught the eye of the publisher of an Amsterdam newspaper, and Jan became a regularly published author." What does *They* in the second sentence stand for?
a. The sea and the harbor patrol
b. De Hartog and the harbor patrol
c. De Hartog and the sea
d. The stories written by Jan

Recognizing Feelings

8. _____ When the head of the Amsterdam Municipal Theater saw Jan for the first time, how did he feel?
a. Startled by Jan's age
b. Awed by Jan's experiences
c. Happy to meet an "old salt"
d. Sad to find a sea mouse

171

9. _____ What have you learned about Jan
de Hartog?
a. He loved playing jokes on
people in authority.
b. He helped many people during
his life.
c. He thought nothing of breaking
the law.
d. He cared only about fame and
money.

Main Idea (10.)_____ What is the main idea of this
story?
a. De Hartog was always a sailor
first, a writer second.
b. Many people like to read
adventure books.
c. De Hartog's books record his
life of adventure.
d. Holland was a brave country
during World War II.

Check your answers with the key.

FA-15 ████████ A NIGHT WITH THE DUCHESS

Find the one correct answer.

Features of
a Short Story

1. _____ What is the setting of the story?
a. The reporter's house
b. A newspaper office
c. A house called Reardon
d. A big city

2. _____ Who are the main characters?
a. Margaret and the Duchess
b. The Duchess and the reporter
c. The Duchess's brother and
Margaret
d. The reporter and her brother

3. _____ What is the tone of this story?
   a. Full of love
   b. Happy
   c. Sad and mysterious
   d. Very funny

4. _____ Which of the following was the most important event in the plot of the story?
   a. A ghost appears in the reporter's bedroom.
   b. The reporter meets Margaret.
   c. The Duchess dies.
   d. The publisher warns the reporter about the Duchess.

Making Inferences

5. _____ Why did the publisher say that Selena was more courageous than he?
   a. He was afraid of his own shadow.
   b. Selena had decided to go to Reardon.
   c. He always liked her stories.
   d. Selena had done many brave things in her life.

Sensory Images

6. _____ Which of your senses is the writer appealing to by saying: "A stiff wind whipped me as I stepped out of my car"?
   a. Sight   c. Touch
   b. Hearing   d. Taste

Recognizing Feelings

7. _____ When Selena heard the Duchess and Margaret outside her room, how did she feel?
   a. Very angry at them
   b. Excited about getting a good story
   c. Very scared about being at Reardon
   d. Very friendly towards the Duchess's brother

173

8. _____ When she was young, the Duchess had only loved money, whereas her brother
   a. cared only about his country.
   b. loved to ride horses.
   c. loved poetry and wanted to help the poor.
   d. was too busy studying to care about anything else.

9. _____ What have you learned about the Duchess?
   a. She was a horrible old woman.
   b. She was too proud to ever admit a mistake.
   c. She was cruel and thoughtless till the day she died.
   d. She felt guilty about her brother's death.

10. _____ What is the main idea of this story?
    a. Reporters live exciting lives.
    b. Never go to a haunted house.
    c. Poets starve and freeze to death.
    d. The Duchess's pride cost her dearly.

Check your answers with the key.

FA-16 ▬▬▬▬▬ THE LAFAYETTE ESCADRILLE

Write *T* if the sentence is true; write *F* if it is false.

1. _____ The following statement is an opinion: "And perhaps there has never been a more exciting war toy than the airplane."

2. _____ Look back to the story to find proof. "Most of the American

pilots who entered the war early were members of the Lafayette Escadrille."

Find the one correct answer.

Important Details

3. _____ When World War I began, how many fighting planes were Germany, France, and England able to put in the air?
a. 200   c. 20,000
b. 2,000   d. 1,000

4. _____ The Red Baron was
a. the owner of a famous circus.
b. a great American hero.
c. a famous cartoon character.
d. an enemy pilot in World War I.

5. _____ The Lafayette Escadrille was the name of
a. the American branch of the French air corps.
b. a type of fighter plane used by the British.
c. the first book written by James Norman Hall.
d. an American general in World War I.

Cause and Effect

6. _____ Aviators were able to shoot each other down because
a. they were very bored just flying around in the air.
b. the generals hadn't yet considered that airplanes could be used as weapons.
c. a man named Fokker figured out how to get machine guns to fire between an airplane's propellers.
d. ground fire couldn't reach the airplanes.

7. _____ "Hall approached the leaders of the Escadrille, who were delighted with his interest. They invited Hall to join the Escadrille and thus experience the story first hand." What does *They* in the second sentence stand for?
   a. Airplanes
   b. Hall and his readers
   c. The French Air Corps
   d. The leaders of the Escadrille

8. _____ What led the author to conclude that Lady Luck actually flew Hall's plane home?
   a. He believes in spirits and ghosts.
   b. The French soldiers who saved Hall saw her.
   c. German fighter planes stopped following Hall.
   d. Somehow, the plane landed while Hall was unconscious.

9. _____ When Hall was captured and a German soldier spoke to him, how did Hall feel?
   a. Scared   c. Hateful
   b. Surprised   d. Jealous

10. _____ What is the main idea of this story?
   a. The invention of the airplane made it possible to fight in the air as well as on the ground.
   b. During World War I, the Germans had the best pilots.
   c. Lady Luck helps American pilots get out of trouble.
   d. The Germans could not afford helmets, so they wore coal buckets.

Check your answers with the key.

Find the one correct answer.

Features of
a Short Story

1. _____ What is the setting of the story?
   a. A dance
   b. A wealthy neighborhood
   c. A church
   d. Dallas

2. _____ Who is the main character?
   a. Lisa
   b. Mrs. Edwards
   c. Mike
   d. Lisa's father

3. _____ Which of the following was the most important event in the plot of the story?
   a. Lisa learns where her father is.
   b. Lisa cleans the church office.
   c. Lisa invites Mike to the spring dance.
   d. Mrs. Connors speaks to Lisa.

4. _____ What is the tone of this story?
   a. Angry   c. Scary
   b. Happy   d. Mysterious

Recognizing
Feelings

5. _____ What did Lisa feel for her sister when Marie gladly accepted clothing given by the church women?
   a. Nervous
   b. Jealous
   c. Disdain
   d. Happy

6. _____ How did Lisa feel when her mother gave the grocer 20 dollars?
   a. Very proud
   b. Angry and cheated
   c. Happy
   d. Guilty

7. _____ Which of your senses is the writer appealing to by saying: "'Some hills,' she thought as she viewed stacks of garbage cans piled high with papers and wine bottles"?
   a. Sight
   b. Hearing
   c. Touch
   d. Taste

Using Context
Clues to Find
Word Meanings

8. _____ Go back to the story to figure out which of the following gives the meaning of *shame*:
   a. A feeling of being very thankful
   b. A painful feeling of disgrace
   c. The wonderful feeling of being loved
   d. The angry feeling of having been betrayed

Predicting
Outcomes

9. _____ What do you think Lisa will do next?
   a. Write a letter to her father
   b. Apologize to her mother
   c. Steal some money from her friend
   d. Make a dress for the dance

Main Idea

10. _____ What is the main idea of this story?
   a. Life is a cruel joke.
   b. Lisa is ashamed of being poor.
   c. Money is the most important thing in life.
   d. Lisa learns that being poor isn't so bad.

Check your answers with the key.

178

Find the one correct answer.

Features of
a Short Story

1. _____ Who are the main characters?
   a. Lisa and her father
   b. Marie and Jerry
   c. Lisa and Hazel
   d. Lisa's father and mother

2. _____ What is the tone of the story?
   a. Funny
   b. Sad
   c. Happy
   d. Mysterious

3. _____ Which of the following was the most important event in the plot of the story?
   a. Lisa gets a letter from her father.
   b. Lisa learns the difference between aft and prow.
   c. Lisa escapes from her father.
   d. Lisa goes to work at the bait shop.

Sensory
Images

4. _____ Which of your senses is the writer appealing to by saying: "The rank smell of the bait shack almost made her sick"?
   a. Sight   c. Touch
   b. Hearing   d. Smell

Using Context
Clues to Find
Word Meanings

5. _____ Go back to the story to figure out which of the following gives the meaning of *smuggling*:
   a. Working in a bait shop
   b. Secretly bringing things into a country
   c. Running away from home
   d. Listening to records

6. _____ "Lisa didn't like the fishermen who came into the place either. They were all older than she, and Lisa was convinced that there wasn't a teen-ager in the vicinity." What does *They* in the second sentence stand for?
   a. Teen-agers
   b. Old people
   c. Fishermen
   d. Lisa's father

7. _____ What have you learned about Lisa's father?
   a. He still loved Lisa's mother very much.
   b. He didn't care about Lisa at all.
   c. He was very courageous.
   d. He was a kind and gentle man.

8. _____ How did Lisa feel after her first week in Nature's Corners?
   a. Very happy
   b. Disappointed and hurt
   c. Guilty and sad
   d. Thrilled and amused

9. _____ When Lisa returned to her mother's place, how did she feel?
   a. Betrayed by her mother and deserted by her father
   b. Relieved to be home, but still ashamed of poverty
   c. Guilty about having left her father and angry at her mother for the run-down apartment
   d. Very happy to have escaped her father and proud to be home

10. _____ What is the main idea of this story?
   a. Lisa learns the awful truth about her father.

180

b. Poor people like Lisa have it rough no matter where they go.
c. There are no fairy godmothers in life.
d. Lisa realizes she's been wrong to object to poverty.

Check your answers with the key.

Find the one correct answer.

Making Comparisons

1. _____ Puccini wrote operas, but he looked like
   a. a sportsman.
   b. the hero of an opera.
   c. a cowboy.
   d. a circus puppet.

Sensory Images

2. _____ Which of your senses is the writer appealing to by saying: "The audience broke into a storm of applause that lasted a full 10 minutes"?
   a. Sight
   b. Hearing
   c. Touch
   d. Taste

Recognizing Feelings

3. _____ How did Puccini feel when the audience applauded him?
   a. Tired   c. Sad
   b. Angry   d. Foolish

Important Details

4. _____ To give Puccini a musical education, his mother
   a. borrowed money.
   b. begged in the streets.
   c. sang to him when he was a baby.
   d. bought a music school.

181

5. _____ Puccini's opera about the American West is based on a play called
a. *Madame Butterfly.*
b. *Can of Corn.*
c. *Girl of the Golden West.*
d. *Little Italy.*

Cause and Effect

6. _____ Puccini thought his wife was a psychic because
a. his friend Caruso had told him so.
b. he started hearing voices.
c. she found a note hidden in his hatband.
d. she told him his future.

Using Context Clues to Find Word Meanings

7. _____ Go back to the story to figure out which of the following gives the meaning of *composer*:
a. Someone who writes music
b. Anyone famous
c. An opera singer
d. A duck hunter

8. _____ Go back to the story to figure out which of the following gives the meaning of *premiere*:
a. Worst performance
b. Last performance
c. First public performance
d. Best scene in an opera

Making Inferences

9. _____ Why did Toscanini put his baton down when he came to the last note Puccini himself had written in *Turandot*?
a. He was too tired to continue.
b. He didn't like the opera.
c. He wanted to honor his dead friend.
d. The audience had walked out on the performance.

Main Idea (10.) _____ What is the main idea of this story?
- a. Puccini liked a pretty face and figure.
- b. All musicians grow up poor.
- c. Opera is boring unless it's sung in English.
- d. Puccini was a great musician and a very interesting man.

Check your answers with the key.

FA-20 ▬▬▬▬▬▬ BLACK WOMAN PILOT FLIES THE FRIENDLY SKIES

Find the one correct answer.

Important Details
1. _____ Of the numerous qualities required of a pilot, which does Tyus say is most important?
- a. Energy
- b. Skill
- c. Confidence
- d. Courtesy

Using Context Clues to Find Word Meanings
2. _____ Go back to the story to figure out which of the following gives the meaning of *career*:
- a. Any kind of job
- b. Positions requiring education, training, and preparation
- c. Jobs that pay well
- d. A promotion to another position at the same company

Cause and Effect
3. _____ Tyus is currently taking a course because
- a. she likes going to school.
- b. she wants a promotion.
- c. everyone takes courses.
- d. she doesn't know what to do next.

4. _____ What led Tyus to work as a part-time pilot for Wheeler Airlines?
   a. She needed the money.
   b. She had finished flight school.
   c. She needed flight time before she could become a pilot for United Airlines.
   d. She did not know how else to spend her vacations and days off.

5. _____ Why are there so few black female pilots?
   a. Black women have been discouraged from entering the field.
   b. There aren't many openings for new pilots.
   c. Becoming a pilot requires much training and preparation.
   d. Black women don't want to become pilots.

6. _____ Which of your senses does this sentence appeal to: "A striking woman in her navy blue uniform, Tyus stops and turns to face them."
   a. Hearing   c. Sight
   b. Touch   d. Smell

7. _____ Some people respond with shock to a black female pilot, whereas
   a. others want to be pilots themselves.
   b. Tyus always dreamed of a career as a pilot.
   c. Tyus had the confidence to become one anyway.
   d. others are surprised but pleased.

Recognizing
Feelings

8. _____ How did Tyus feel when she took
her parents for a joy ride in the
sky?
a. Proud   c. Angry
b. Sad   d. Scared

Predicting
Outcomes

9. _____ What do you think Tyus will do
after she receives her promotion
to first officer?
a. Start a flight school for pilots
b. Work to receive a promotion to
captain
c. Give up being a pilot and
become a teacher instead
d. Spend more time with her family

Main Idea

(10.) _____ What is the main idea of this
story?
a. Becoming a pilot takes time,
energy, and hard work.
b. With ambition, confidence,
and hard work, black women
can have successful careers as
pilots.
c. Because of affirmative action,
there are more black pilots
now than there were in the
1960s.
d. Flight school is very expensive.

Check your answers with the key.

FA-1	FA-2	FA-3	FA-4	FA-5
1. T	1. b	1. F	1. c	1. b
2. T	2. c	2. c	2. c	2. b
3. b	3. b	3. a	3. c	3. d
4. c	4. b	4. d	4. d	4. a
5. c	5. b	5. b	5. b	5. c
6. d	6. a	6. a	6. c	6. a
7. a	7. a	7. c	7. c	7. a
8. b	8. c	8. b	8. a	8. c
9. b	9. d	9. b	9. c	9. c
10. a	10. b	10. d	10. c	10. c

FA-6	FA-7	FA-8	FA-9	FA-10
1. c	1. d	1. b	1. b	1. d
2. d	2. d	2. a	2. c	2. d
3. a	3. c	3. c	3. c	3. a
4. c	4. d	4. b	4. a	4. c
5. c	5. a	5. d	5. F	5. c
6. d	6. b	6. a	6. T	6. d
7. c	7. c	7. d	7. c	7. c
8. c	8. c	8. a	8. a	8. b
9. a	9. b	9. a	9. c	9. c
10. b	10. a	10. c	10. b	10. c

FA-11	FA-12	FA-13	FA-14	FA-15
1. d	1. b	1. b	1. b	1. c
2. d	2. d	2. c	2. c	2. b
3. b	3. b	3. b	3. c	3. c
4. c	4. b	4. c	4. a	4. a
5. c	5. d	5. d	5. a	5. b
6. c	6. F	6. c	6. b	6. c
7. a	7. c	7. a	7. d	7. b
8. c	8. c	8. c	8. a	8. c
9. d	9. c	9. d	9. b	9. d
10. b	10. a	10. c	10. c	10. d

FA-16	FA-17	FA-18	FA-19	FA-20
1. T	1. d	1. a	1. b	1. c
2. T	2. a	2. b	2. b	2. b
3. b	3. a	3. c	3. d	3. b
4. d	4. a	4. d	4. b	4. c
5. a	5. c	5. b	5. c	5. a
6. c	6. b	6. c	6. c	6. c
7. d	7. a	7. b	7. a	7. d
8. d	8. b	8. b	8. c	8. a
9. b	9. a	9. b	9. c	9. b
10. a	10. b	10. a	10. d	10. b